DEDICATION

I dedicate this book to my Heavenly Father, who has given me the wisdom, and knowledge in putting the right words and ideas where they need to be. I also give my Lord the thanks for giving me the breath of life and the many years to be able to experience His presence during each and every step on this journey.

Contents

Introduction

It is my personal belief that God is an amazing God, and a loving Father. One of the many things that a loving Father enjoys doing is to spend time with his children.

As I continue my journey with God through what I call life, I've learned that God really enjoys our company and what we think and what our plans are, and accompanies us on our journey.

Because God is also love, He likes to participate in our travels, and when we unintentionally take a wrong turn in life, which happens more often than not, God makes His presence known to us. Since our Heavenly Father knows the ending from the beginning, He speaks to our spirit, and directs our footsteps on to the path that has a better future for His children, when we listen.

This journey with God are exerts or glimpses into the journey that I have personally experienced, and how God has met me on the path of life wherever I was, and spoke with me, and walked with me, and helped me to understand who He is, and how much He loves me.

It is my desire for the reader to come into that place that walking and talking with God are not a complicated, religious formula, but an everyday, normal occurrence, as easy as breathing in and breathing out, and that God is truly on your side, and wants only the best for you. God wants you to know that He will meet you in every aspect of your life, in your home, with your family and in your business.

God truly is an amazing Father, and if given the opportunity, He will reveal to each and every one of you the deeper secrets and mysteries of His very heart.

What to do, What to do

The other day I was sitting around the table, and planning my next three months' worth of agendas. I remember talking to myself, asking the many questions, when do I travel north, how long do I stay there before heading south, when do I go to Florida, what about our return to Europe and the Middle East, how do I fit those into our plans and how do I tie all those plans together? I remember very clearly asking myself the question, 'What to do, what to do.'

I've come to the conclusion that life is like a juggling act. There are so many things we need to keep in motion all the time, such as our social life, spiritual life, church life, personal life, family life, professional working life, and I'm sure if you're a Mom or a Dad, there are other concerns that need to be considered such as the children's soccer practice, swimming, baseball, homework, school activities, not to mention family cooking, friends dropping by, co-workers stopping over, quiet time, and family time and the list goes on and on.

It's amazing that we are able to balance a few of these without going off the deep end, not to mention some of us have to balance all of these.

And then, in the middle of preparing our plans, the question pops up how do I really know if it's the Lord's plans or my plans? What do I do when I'm right in the middle of securing the plans that I've worked out, figured out in some cases paid for in advance, only to find that it was all my plans and cleverness all along because the plans seemed so right? What to do, what to do. Do I stop go back to step one? Do I press on and continue along the path? How do I incorporate God into the equation or formula so my ending will be a happy ending?

Jeremiah 29:11 tells us, "I know the plans that I have for you says the Lord." The problem many times is, that we know the plans that we have for ourselves, and His plans for us, and our plans for us are not one and the same.

Example, I remember once Norma wanted to go to Texas for a convention, and she purchased the airline ticket. All her plans were in order, and everything was set for her to leave. The only problem was; it was her plans and not the Lord's plans, and a few days before leaving she got cold feet and didn't want to go.

Talk about a game of mental ping-pong. I have to go because I have the ticket, but I don't want to go. I need to go because I don't want to waste the money, but I don't feel this is of the Lord. On and on this battle went until I said, give me the tickets. I took Norma and the tickets outside to the backyard, offered them up to the Lord as a burnt sacrifice, repented for not checking in with the Lord first and put a fire to them, end of debate.

How many times do we find ourselves in this situation? What happens when we do that with a new house or a car or moving to another city? The price of an airline ticket is a far cry from a new car or buying a new house or tuition to a certain college far away.

So what's the solution? How do we make sure, to the best of our understanding that it's part of the Lord's plans, and not our plans that we have spiritualized so we can justify the investment, or time or action that we are going to put to the adventure?

The solution can be summed up in a few verses that basically all say the same thing.

"Then you will call on me and come and pray to me, and I will listen to you. You will seek me and find me when you seek me with all your heart." Jeremiah 29:12, 13.

"Call to me and I will answer you and tell you great and unsearchable things you do not know." Jeremiah 33:3.

"But if from there you seek the LORD your God, you will find him if you seek him with all your heart and with all your soul." Deuteronomy 4:29, and finally, the answer in simple, plain English, "Trust in the Lord with all your heart and lean not on your own understanding, in all your ways submit to him, and he will make your paths straight." Proverbs 3:5, 6.

You know, when we set out to make plans for life, we really hope it will turn out okay. The best we can do is hope it will be okay, because we don't know the future, but we are told in Isaiah 42:9 concerning God, "See, the former things have taken place, and new things I declare, before they spring into being I announce them to you." God knows the best plans for our life. God also knows what the next step we are to take is, and the name of the school we are to attend, or the next city we are to visit. As we get involved in God's business, God will get involved in our business, and all we have to do, is what we are told to do in Matthew 7:7 "Ask and it will be given to you, seek and you will find, knock and the door will be opened to you." If you want to know the next step in your life, ask Him, and He will tell you, and also give you a peace that exceeds all understanding as you make the decision.

Prayer, Lord, help me to trust You for all my decisions, and to check in with You before I make any plans that I'm not completely sure about.

Get Up

When I was just a kid in grade school, living in New York City, almost every morning during school season, I would hear the most wonderful sound of my mother as she greeted me first thing in the morning with 'Get Up'. And if you were anything like me, you usually heard it at least 3 to 4 times. And again if you were anything like me, I knew around the fourth time based on the tone in my mom's voice that I had just pushed the last button, and it really was time to get up.

Once I graduated from school and entered the Air Force, I thought the wonderful ring of 'Get Up' was far behind me, but was I mistaken. All of us airmen would meet on the physical fitness field for what we called physical education, which started with push-ups, running, jumping into the water and ending with push-ups. For those who were in the service, remember boot camp? There were probably 75 airmen on the ground doing push-ups and that type of exercise was always difficult for me, and after maybe 10 of them, I would just lay upon the ground. With a loud booming voice that could be heard in the next state, I would hear, Budweiser, Get Up. I have no idea why they nicknamed me Budweiser; I never consumed any type of alcohol when I was in the service, and maybe some wine nowadays for Shabbat.

Anyway, it seemed the familiar sound of Get Up followed me from childhood to wherever I went.

This morning I was reading through the book of Joshua in chapter 7, and twice I hear God speak to Joshua, and tell him to Get Up. You have no idea how happy I was to know that I wasn't the only one singled out to get up.

So what's the setting for this scene? Joshua and the army of the living God have been on the move, and taking all the land that God tells them He is giving them. They just defeated the large city of Jericho with a loud shout, and their next city is Ai, which is really a nothing to brag about size city. As a matter of fact, one of the soldiers tells Joshua that maybe 3000 soldiers are all that's needed to do the clean-up job. So Joshua sends 3000 soldiers, and they get their clocks cleaned so badly that we are told their hearts were like water, meaning they were really scared.

Joshua was told by God that none of the accursed things of the city of Jericho was to be taken, and all valuables were to be placed in God's treasury. The problem was that behind Joshua's back, and without his knowing, one of the soldiers in the army took some of the accursed things. If you read chapter 7 in Joshua, you will see what trinkets were taken, and why 36 men had to die, and the army put to defeat by an insignificant city according to Joshua 7.

We see Joshua on his face before the Lord praying, whining and complaining to God and asking Him, God, what's up? Why did You allow this to happen? And God, the creator of the universe, the Almighty One, The One who knows the ending from the beginning speaks these famous words to Joshua in Joshua 7:10 "But the LORD said to Joshua, "Get up! Why are you lying on your face like this?" What God says is, 'Joshua I know you can pray, but I didn't tell you to pray I told you to fight, Get Up.'

Disobedience or sin brings its own curse. Genesis 4:7 states, "If you do what is right, will you not be accepted? But if you do not do what is right, sin is crouching at your door, it desires to have you, but you must rule over it." By the way, in ancient Hebrew the concept of sin desiring you can be likened to a leopard in a tree, ready to pounce on the prey walking unknowingly past the tree, and not knowing the predator has its eye on every move you are making.

5

The issue becomes, how many times have we either knowingly or unknowingly sinned against a Holy and Just God, and when the consequences of our actions over take us, we fall upon our knees and ask, why God?

The answer should be evident; sin will take you further than you ever intended to go, cost you more than you ever intended to pay, keep you there longer than you ever intended to stay and hurt more people than you ever intended it to hurt.

When there's sin in the camp, everyone pays. The Book of Joshua 7:1 tells us, "But the Israelites were unfaithful in regard to the devoted things, Achan son of Karmi, the son of Zimri, the son of Zerah, of the tribe of Judah, took some of them. So the Lord's anger burned against Israel. God even tells Joshua "Israel has sinned, they have violated my covenant, which I commanded them to keep. They have taken some of the devoted things, they have stolen, they have lied, and they have put them with their own possessions." Joshua 7:11

So what do we do after we have sinned, and we are reaping that which we have sown? What do we do now that the consequences of our actions have caught up to us, and don't be fooled, they will catch up to you. Your actions on earth are broadcasted in heaven? Nothing in all creation is hidden from God's sight.

Everything is uncovered, and laid bare before the eyes of him to whom we must give an account, "Nothing in all creation is hidden from God's sight. Everything is uncovered and laid bare before the eyes of him to whom we must give an account." Hebrews 4:13. Psalm 11:4 states, "He, observes everyone on earth, his eyes examine them." If God repeats Himself more than once, it should be noted as really important, and in Psalm 33:13 "From heaven the LORD looks down and sees all mankind,"

So again, what do we do after we have sinned, and we are reaping that which we have sown? We are told the solution for Joshua after he asked God the same question can be found in Joshua 7:13 "Go, consecrate the people. Tell them, consecrate yourselves in preparation for tomorrow, for this is what the LORD, the God of Israel, says, "There are devoted things among you, Israel. You cannot stand against your enemies until you remove them.""

That word sanctify in Hebrew is 'Qadash,' and means to make yourself morally and ceremonially clean. We know it as purify or consecrate.

What that meant for Joshua was, to get up, get rid of the accursed thing, and destroy all evidence of those who were responsible for bringing sin into the camp. For us today, it means, Get Up, get rid of the sin in your life, turn from the sinful action that is hurting so many people, go to the foot of the cross and ask for forgiveness, repent, just don't be sorry that you got caught. Will you be forgiven? According to God's word, we are, "If we confess our sins, he is faithful and just and will forgive us our sins and purify us from all unrighteousness." 1 John 1:9. Once more, "Repent, then, and turn to God, so that your sins may be wiped out, that times of refreshing may come from the Lord." Acts 3:19

So what do we do? We get up, we ask God to forgive us; we forgive ourselves, and we ask those that we have knowingly hurt to forgive us and press on to what God has for us.

By the way, depending on how bad the sin was, when God forgives us, we are forgiven but the consequences of that sin may linger a life time. If you want to know what God considers to be a sin, I would suggest that you read His book, and He will very gladly let you know what He wants you to do, and what He doesn't want you to do, and that's what I call a loving Heavenly Father.

Prayer, Father, I know that I sin but don't make a habit of sinning, and I ask You to help me in my weakness that I might be an over comer in the areas of my weakness.

Watch What You Declare

The other day I was doing my devotional in the book of Job 3:25, and it jumped from the page at me, and really hit home.

One version says, "For the thing which I greatly feared is come upon me, and that which I was afraid of is come unto me-KJV."

Another version puts it this way, "For the dreaded thing that I feared has happened to me, what caused me to worry has engulfed me-ISV."

My favorite version tells me, "What I fear most overtakes me. What I dread happens to me-GW."

Kind of reminds me of a story someone told me about a Florida football coach, who got a phone call in the middle of the night from the local police station. They told the coach that twelve of his best players were out drinking and having a great time, and they all got into trouble and were all locked up waiting for his arrival. He told the police officer at the duty station that he had always feared that his players would get into trouble, and the thought of that has haunted him for years, and now the very thing which he has feared has come upon him.

I'm sure many parents or spouses do exactly what this coach did, or for that matter, what Job did. They rehearse in their minds the problems or troubles or accidents that will one day happen to their children or their better half or to themselves. I'm equally sure that each and every one of us rehearse in our minds the cold or flu that we're going to get or come down with.

9

How many times have you experienced a minor tickle in your throat, and your confession is, 'I'm coming down with a cold, or I'm gonna get sick; I can just feel it?' It doesn't matter how you justify it, that's a negative confession, and it doesn't belong in the mouth or thoughts of a born-again believer.

And you know these negative confessions aren't limited just how we are feeling physically. How many times have you heard someone say, 'I'll never get that job or that promotion will never be mine, I'm not educated enough.'

I mentioned this to someone once, and they told me, 'Well that's just human nature and natural.' Well, I'm sorry, but if you are a child of the living God, you are not natural and negative confessions are not part of who we are. Proverbs tells us "The tongue has the power of life and death, and those who love it will eat its fruit." Proverbs 18:21

Have you ever noticed how we not only entertain negative thoughts or worse case scenarios, but we even seem to put the event on replay so it keeps going over and over in our minds, and in many cases, the negative event seems to get larger with each replay? Not only that, but most of the time the automatic replays are in the early-morning hours when we are tossing and turning, when we should be sleeping.

Recently, I heard someone say, 'Whatever you are afraid of you will not be able to conquer.' To make matters worse, we often times make a mountain of out a mole hill. You know the meaning; we make something very large out of something that was supposed to be very small.

The problem is, as we continue to focus on the negative and to think about it all the time, we often times experience what Job experienced and that is, the things which he has feared have come upon him. Why? Because Job like many of us have summoned the things that do not yet exist as though they already do, and they become a reality in our lives.

Scripture tells us, we can call the things which are not as if they were, or we can call the things which are as if they were not. What does that mean? If you need a job and don't have a job, you can call it into existence through the power of Jesus Christ, or if there's sickness in your body you can call it as if it weren't there, again in the power of Jesus Christ.

Truly Proverbs 21:23 is so very true, "Those who guard their mouths and their tongues keep themselves from calamity." Again, Proverbs 18:21 "The tongue has the power of life and death, and those who love it will eat its fruit."

If we really applied Colossians 3:17 "And whatever you do, whether in word or deed, do it all in the name of the Lord Jesus, giving thanks to God the Father through him." If we did that, we wouldn't be making so many negative confessions. Don't get me wrong, I'm not saying we never get sick, or we don't lose a job, or something bad doesn't happen to us. That's a fact, but we don't have to go through the entire day complaining and whining and telling ourselves how bad it is, and that this will last forever.

There's a big difference between fact and truth. It may be a fact that you have a bad cold, but it's not true that it's the end of the world for you. It may be a fact that you lost your job, but it's not true that you are a failure.

My friends, you are so much more than just a name; you are a child of the living God with an inheritance from your Heavenly Father; you have a destiny; you are seated in heavenly places, or as I'm so fond of telling people when asked how am I, I'm too blessed to be cursed, too rich to be poor and too healed to be sick.

It's amazing, Paul said, 'the things I want to do, I don't do and yet the very things I don't want to do are the things I do.' Do you know we are no different than what Paul is describing here? Why do I say that? We are all aware of scripture that speaks about the tongue, "Whoever would love life and see good days must keep their tongue from evil and their lips from deceitful speech" 1 Peter 3:10, or "Do you see someone who speaks in haste? There is more hope for a fool than for them." Proverbs 29:20

We know how we should speak but do we do it, not really. We know that negative thoughts are from the enemy but do we come against them, not really; as a matter of fact, most of the time we entertain them more than we should, and if that's not bad enough, we often times even agree with them.

Stop taking possession of what doesn't belong to you especially with your words. Don't take possessive pride in your problems, stop saying, my backache, my sickness, my lack of education.

Here's an example, we start to get a runny nose, and the confession of our mouth is, 'I'm coming down with a bad cold,' and then we agree with it by taking all kinds of pills and it's nothing more than your nose running. Why not take it to the Lord and see what He says, although He already said He sent His word to heal your sickness and diseases.

Once again, I'm not saying you're not coming down with a cold; you may very well have cold, bad things happen to good people, what I am saying is, 'Don't be quick to agree with your feelings or your thoughts.' The enemy usually speaks in the third person, I'm a failure; I have a sickness, and I'll never amount to much. In other words, check with the throne before you believe the lie and confess to something that doesn't belong to you, and certainly don't call the things that are not as if they are, especially if they are things that you don't want for your life.

If you must confess anything, why not start to confess what God has already said about you. In every situation in your life, there is something positive that God has already spoken over you, now what we need to do is declare it, proclaim it, and confess it.

Remember my friends, a declaration is confessing what you already have, not what you want. When you travel overseas or to a foreign country and when you return to this country, you pass through the customs department and are asked to fill out a declaration form of what you have in your possession, not what you would have liked to get.

Prayer, Father, help me to declare what You have already said I own, and not only declare it but to walk in it as well.

God of All

I was reading through the book of Daniel, and I was amazed by the pride and arrogance of both Kings Nebuchadnezzar and his son Belshazzar. I was really drawn to Daniel 4:30 when King Nebuchadnezzar declares, "Is not this the great Babylon I have built as the royal residence, by my mighty power and for the glory of my majesty?"

It would seem the memory of kings and the memories of the children of God are indeed very short lived. It was only one year earlier that King Nebuchadnezzar had a dream, and the meaning of the dream was explained by Daniel, and the king was told, because of your pride and arrogance you will spend 7 years as an animal eating grass like oxen. Daniel even goes so far as to reveal to the king what might be the answer to the prophecy, and that is found in Daniel 4:25 "You will be driven away from people and will live with the wild animals, you will eat grass like the ox and be drenched with the dew of heaven. Seven times will pass by for you until you acknowledge that the Most High is sovereign over all kingdoms on earth and gives them to anyone He wishes." However, once again, the memory of kings is very short lived.

What was it that restored to the king his kingdom, and the mind of a man, and the glory of his kingdom, his honor and splendor? It's when King Nebuchadnezzar came to that place where he says in Daniel 4:34, 35 "But at the end of that period, I, Nebuchadnezzar, raised my eyes toward heaven and my reason returned to me, and I blessed the Most High and praised and honored Him who lives forever, For His dominion is an everlasting dominion, and His kingdom endures from generation to generation."

14

Sometimes we look at what the Lord has allowed us to accumulate from wealth, to education, to material increase, or even family members, and we as King Nebuchadnezzar get a little proud or arrogant and declare to ourselves or to others, 'Is this not great what I have done, what I have accumulated which I myself have built as a royal residence by the might of my power or my education or my wealth and all for the glory of my majesty.'

Many might be saying to themselves, 'I would never say something like that.' The truth is, if you don't give God the glory, then you are keeping it for yourself. You might be saying, that's not true, but I ask you, 'Who do you give thanks to?' Who do you thank for all the things you have accumulated? It's stated in Ecclesiastes 5:19 "Moreover, when God gives someone wealth and possessions, and the ability to enjoy them, to accept their lot and be happy in their toil, this is a gift of God," also in Ephesians 5:20 "Always giving thanks to God the Father for everything, in the name of our Lord Jesus Christ."

That last verse tells us to give thanks to God for everything, and to my understanding, everything means everything.

Another word for everything is, entirety or all. In the Slang Dictionary at onlineslangdictionary.com it means, the whole shebang, or the whole kit and caboodle, or the whole enchilada. In other words, everything we own, who we are and hope to become is a gift from our Heavenly Father.

We were all taught as children to say thank you when anyone gave us a gift, and our Heavenly Father deserves a thank you for all the gifts He has given us.

Although you may not be out in the green pasture eating plants like a wild animal, the Lord can very easily cause your excess to dry up, or your wealth to disappear, or your entire social, financial or medical situation to change for the worse because of pride and arrogance.

Saying thank you is an act of humility, and humility comes easy to a humble person. In James 4:10 it tells us, "Humble yourselves before the Lord, and he will lift you up," and Psalm 25:9 "He guides the humble in what is right and teaches them his way."

So many times in scripture we are reminded to give God all the glory for all He has done. Twice Jesus tells us to do something in remembrance of Him.

When it comes to the treasures we have, it would be a good idea to remember Deuteronomy 8:18 "But remember the LORD your God, for it is he who gives you the ability to produce wealth." Other translations use the word success but regardless of the word, be it wealth or success or prosperity, it is God who has given us the ability, and all things belong to Him.

Everything that King Nebuchadnezzar owned, his cities, lands, mansions, gold, wealth, armies even his royal position, it was all because of Almighty God, and if he had only heeded the words of Daniel when he told the king 'Break away now from your sins by doing righteousness and from your iniquities by showing mercy to the poor and bless the Most High and praise and honor Him who lives forever, for His dominion is an everlasting dominion.'

Prayer, Father, help me to give credit where credit is due, and You get all the credit for everything, all the time, and in every place.

☐

God Allows U-Turns

I was reading through the book of Isaiah, and I came upon that familiar verse in Isaiah 35:8 where it tells us, "And a highway will be there, it will be called the Way of Holiness, it will be for those who walk on that Way. The unclean will not journey on it, wicked fools will not go about on it." Strange as it may seem, it triggered a funny thought in my mind, and I said to myself, 'How come we drive on a parkway and park in a driveway?'

But then I remembered the many, many times I have been driving the wrong way on a road, and knew I had made a wrong turn and was going in the wrong direction. As I mentioned, I knew I was going in the wrong direction but there seems to be something in the chemical make-up of men that refuses to allow them to ask directions, or at least many men.

Sometimes I wonder about my driver reasoning abilities that tell me, 'If I continue to drive in the wrong direction why do you think that suddenly I will arrive at my destination.' What's desperately needed is a U-turn on this highway, so I can start heading back in the right direction towards what I know will take me to my final destination

The older I get; it seems I'm making more U-turns on what use to be familiar paths and the more reasonable and acceptable the U-turns seem to be.

You know my friends, many of the U-turns are not only on physical roads but on spiritual roads as well. That highway found in Isaiah, which is called the Way of Holiness is a spiritual road and how many times have we as believers taken a short cut, or a detour on that Way of Holiness, only to find ourselves in a desolate or barren place? How many of us have been there and refused to ask for directions, or have decided to continue with the journey thinking we will end up where God wants us to be. As long as we continue walking in disobedience, which is the same as taking a detour on the Way of Holiness you will probably never get to the destination God has for you, the way He planned it for you.

God wants us to continue going straight on the path He has set for us, and we decide to take a left or right turn because it will get us there quicker. It's very much like the saying, 'I don't have time to do it right the first time but always have time to do it right the second time.'

Here's the good news my friends, God allows U-turns. If your life is going in the wrong direction, God allows U-turns with your life. If your marriage is heading in the wrong direction, God allows U-turns in your marriage. If your job, or your physical condition, or your children, or your spiritual condition is headed in the wrong direction, and you know if it's not what it used to be, God allows U-turns. Not only that, God also allows you to ask for directions on how to get back on the Way of Holiness so you can continue on your journey with Him.

There are so many parallels between our spiritual walk with God, and the highways that we drive on. Have you ever noticed that during a major snow storm, like what many have experienced, that the major roads are clear, and the side roads are still hazardous to travel? Have you ever seen a vehicle broken down on a major highway, and the roadside assistance vehicle is there to help with the problem? I've never seen the roadside assistance vehicle leave the highway to help a stranded or broken vehicle that has left the major highway.

That is called God's protection. Not only does God allow U-turns but He also has His ministering angels who watch over us as we travel. He also has rest areas on many of the well-traveled highways. Areas where you can stop and be refreshed, rest a while, even walk around and pick up a map for the area that you're in. Maps are great, especially if you are not familiar with the way to go. Even the Lord wants us to know where we are during our travels, "Set up road signs, put up guideposts. Take note of the highway, the road that you take." Jeremiah 31:21

It's exactly the same with the Way of Holiness, or what I like to think of as our spiritual walk. As we journey along with God, there are rest areas where we can be refreshed, Isaiah 28:12 informs us that God has told his people, "To whom he said, "This is the resting place, let the weary rest" and, "This is the place of repose," but they would not listen." We can also get directions for our walk with those who have travelled the road more often. Proverbs 13:20 tells us, "Walk with the wise and become wise, associate with fools and get in trouble," and Proverbs 9:9 "Instruct the wise and they will be wiser still, teach the righteous and they will add to their learning."

It's absolutely amazing that the Almighty God; creator of all things wants us to make a U-turn during our journey if our life is not what it should be in Him. We read in Zechariah 1:3 "Therefore tell the people, this is what the LORD Almighty says, 'Return to me,' declares the LORD Almighty, and I will return to you, says the LORD

19

Almighty." We see this in the life of the prodigal son. He left the Way of Holiness for a detour in life that didn't turn out the way the son thought it would turn out. Somewhere it was decided, and usually that somewhere is the bottom of the barrel of life that a U-turn was needed to get back to where and how it used to be. In keeping with Zechariah, the son returned to the father, and the father returned to the son.

My friends, if your life is not going the way it was at first, and you seem to be taking a detour with the Lord, if you feel that you left the Way of Holiness for a secondary road, God allows U-turns with your life, and is already waiting for your return. Today is the perfect day to stop, turn around, and head back to that place where you can get the rest, comfort and protection that your spirit yearns for.

Prayer, Oh Lord, many times I have made wrong turns in life, and tried to figure out the right path on my own, help me to seek Your face and Your directions for my life.

Expect the Unexpected

You know, I've spoken with people that have had so many blessings in their lives that just seem to keep on coming, and although thankful, their attitude was; with all these blessings, something has to change; they can't just continue. In other words, they were expecting the unexpected.

That attitude causes me to question their depth of spiritual understanding or the faithfulness of God in their lives. I mean doesn't Deuteronomy 28:2 tell us "And all these blessings shall come upon you and overtake you, if you obey the voice of the LORD your God." Another version makes it even clearer when it tells us, "All these blessings will come on you and accompany you if you obey the LORD your God." I don't read anywhere in scripture where it tells us we have a quota and once that quota is filled all the blessings stop. The word accompany means, to escort or to go along with.

What we see is that the blessings of God are conditional. In other words, if you do that, I will do this. God says if you listen to Me and obey Me than I will pour blessings on you in abundance, and those blessings will go with you. Go with me where, you might be asking? Well, I'm glad you asked; the answer is found in Deuteronomy 28:3-8 where God tells us, "You will be blessed in the city and blessed in the country. The fruit of your womb will be blessed, and the crops of your land and the young of your livestock, the calves of your herds and the lambs of your flocks. Your basket and your kneading trough will be blessed. You will be blessed when you come in and blessed when you go out. The Lord will grant that the enemies who rise up against you will be defeated before you. They will come at you from one direction but flee from you in seven. The Lord will send a blessing on your barns and on everything you put your hand to. The Lord your God will bless you in the land he is giving you."

Let's not forget the Lord is the One who sends the blessings; they are His gifts to us. What exactly is a blessing? That is another teaching for another time, but I want to say that the blessings of God brings about a complete turnabout in your life. The best way to explain that is by giving you an example. In Esther 5:14 it states, Then his wife Zeresh and all his friends said to him, meaning Haman, "Let a gallows fifty cubits high be made, and in the morning tell the king to have Mordecai hanged upon it. Then go joyfully with the king to the feast." This idea pleased Haman, and he had the gallows made.

My friends that was a death sentence for Mordecai, and there was nothing that he could have earthly done to stop this death sentence. I'm sure there are many out there today that have received a report that seems like there is nothing earthly that you can do about it. A report from the doctor that there is no hope, a job that the boss said you are about to lose, and you depend on that job to support and feed your family or maybe your spouse informed you that I don't love you anymore, there are so many reports that have a finality to them and there doesn't seem to be a way

22

out of the negative report, much like Mordecai. But you see my friends; it isn't over until it's over. We read in Esther 7:10 "So they hanged Haman on the very gallows that he had prepared for Mordecai. The king's anger was then pacified."

That is what I like to call a Mordecai moment. One moment you are expecting the worst possible outcome, and the next moment everything is completely turned around, and you are delivered, but not only delivered but much better than when you went into the experience.

Not only does the doctor change his mind from no hope, to 'I can't find any reason for you to even be in the hospital; you are as healthy as a teenager,' or the boss tells you, 'I've had a change of mind, and you are not fired but I want to give you a raise and a promotion,' or your spouse tells you, 'I wasn't in my right mind and please forgive me for those hurtful words; the truth is I could never live without you; you are my everything and a gift from the Lord.'

It boils down to whose report will you believe. It has nothing to do with feelings, or warm fuzzies, or my gut is telling me this, but it has everything to do with what has God told you, and why would you listen to another report anyway.

If another report doesn't confirm or support what God has already told you, you have no right to listen to it. When God tells you something, there is a period after what He says, not a comma, and it's never a run-on sentence. God says what He means, and means what He says, and He will see it through to completion with a complete total victory in the life of the receiver.

There used to be a bumper sticker that said, 'God said it, I believe it, that settles it.' I have to disagree with that bumper sticker, it should have said, God said it that settles it. It makes no difference what you believe, because what you believe doesn't change the truth only your relationship to the truth, and God is the absolute, final truth of all that matters here on earth, in the heavens, under the earth, in the eternal past, the present, and the eternal future.

Prayer, as the father of the paraplegic said, Lord, I believe, help my unbelief. I also say Lord help my unbelief, my lack of trust and my lack of love when it comes to You.

A Bird in a Cage

There was an album by 'The Walls' called 'A Bird in a Cage,' and it brought to mind something I use to do when I was a teenager. I use to get a small flat box, prop it up with a stick that I had tied a string to. I put bird seed all around the front of the box, and some inside the area under the propped box, and waited for a bird to show up. Usually, it didn't take long. Mind you, I was only about ten feet from the box holding the string in my hand, waiting. If the bird had looked around, it would have seen me, but I guess food was more important than anything, and the idea of being caught never entered its mind. After a few minutes, the bird eventually came to the box, and although a little skittish, it nevertheless, followed the seed trail right under the box. I waited about 15 seconds and pulled the string. Guess who caught a bird? After my victory, I let the bird go only to try it again with another bird, and it usually always was a success. Of course, I let every bird go free. I didn't want the birds only the victory of catching them.

According to Donna Kay, Yahoo Contributing Editor, she says, 'Our feathered friends have truly amazing eyesight. In fact, the clarity with which they see the world is similar to that of humans. But birds actually process the information they see much faster than humans, and they can spot movement much better.'

25

Obviously, the bird's eyesight is much better than its ability to reason themselves out of trouble or a deceptive sticky situation. If I had a very large box that was propped up with a stick and a piece of rope tied to it, and I put money on the ground and a few dollars under the box, and you could see me very clearly, I doubt you would walk under the box because you would reason and rightly so, that it was a trap, and you would run the other way. In Amos 3:5 God tells us, "Does a bird swoop down to a trap on the ground when no bait is there? Does a trap spring up from the ground if it has not caught anything?"

We are basically told the same thing in Psalm 140:5, "The arrogant have hidden a snare for me, they have spread out the cords of their net and have set traps for me along my path."

What is God telling us in Amos 3:5 when it says, "Does a bird swoop down to a trap on the ground when no bait is there? Does a trap spring up from the ground if it has not caught anything?"

He's telling us that the enemy has all sorts of deceptive baits, and he wants to trap or ensnare us with these temptations. However, Jesus tells us in Matthew 10:16 "I am sending you out like sheep among wolves. Therefore be as shrewd as snakes and as innocent as doves." Why would He say snakes or serpents? Because in Genesis 3:1 it tells us, "Now the serpent was craftier than any of the wild animals the LORD God had made. He said to the woman, "Did God really say, 'You must not eat from any tree in the garden?'" Another word for serpent is Shining One, which comes from the Hebrew root word "Nachash" which means one who practices divination and omens.

God is saying, we, the children of God are to be more cunning, more clever more crafty and wiser than the Shining One who practice's divination which is the mode, and techniques of the evil one.

When the evil one baits his trap to ensnare us, we should be wiser and more cleaver so as not to get trapped in his cage. You see, once you are in a cage you are no longer free. Yet Galatians 5:1 says, "It is for freedom that Christ has set us free. Stand firm, then, and do not let yourselves be burdened again by a yoke of slavery," John 8:36 agrees with this when it tells us, "So if the Son sets you free, you will be free indeed."

If we are wiser than the deceitful one, we will be aware of his tactics and able to withstand the temptations he lays out for us. When that happens, the second part of Amos 3:5 becomes a reality, which tells us, "Does a trap spring up from the ground if it has not caught anything?" The answer is no of course not, there's nothing or anyone to catch because we didn't take his bait, and the cage is empty.

Is it because of your great ability to know the tactics of the enemy that you were able to avoid being caught or trapped? I don't think so, 2 Peter 2:9 reveals the reason we can avoid the enemies' temptations, it tells us, "If this is so, then the Lord knows how to rescue the godly from trials and to hold the unrighteous for punishment on the Day of Judgment." You see the Lord takes care of His own. Is that biblical? You bet, Ephesians 1:14 says, "Who is a deposit guaranteeing our inheritance until the redemption of those who are God's possession, to the praise of his glory," and Revelation 5:9 confirms this, "And they sang a new song, saying, "You are worthy to take the scroll and to open its seals, because you were slain, and with your blood you purchased for God persons from every tribe and language and people and nation."

It is God who enables us to be cleaver, wise, and cunning enough to avoid the fiery darts of the enemy, and the temptations laid before us, so we will not be caught in the enemies' trap or cage.

We started with a song about a bird in a cage, and we end with a song about a bird, only this song is by ABBA, and it tells us, Una Paloma Blanca, I'm just a bird in the sky Una Paloma Blanca over the mountains I fly no one can take my freedom away.

Remember that my friends, no one, not even the evil one can take your God-given freedom away, and don't you give it away either.

Prayer, Father, help me to be aware of the traps and deceptions of the evil one, and direct my steps into that which is pleasing to You.

A Scriptural Prayer for My Friends

This section is a little different than the others. It's something for you to receive in your Spirit, and agree with if you feel it's for you, and your family and friends.

Often times I find myself sitting by the window or in front of my computer, and the Lord directs my attention to prayer and especially for my friends.

Norma and I have been blessed with hundreds of friends all around the world, so praying for each of you can really be a challenge, especially since we have no idea what each of you are going through at the very moment I begin to pray for you.

If I had to depend on my own thoughts and feelings to drum up the right words for each and every one of you, I would really be up against a wall, and my prayers would fall short of what would be needed at the exact moment of prayer. Thank God the Lord showed me that if I pray scriptural prayers for you, the prayers would never fall short, and would be as timeless as the Word of God itself, and the prayers would be jam-packed with power from on high, and able to do what God intends for His Word to do.

How can you be certain that your scriptural prayers will accomplish what you pray? I'm told in John 1:1 "In the beginning was the Word, and the Word was with God, and the Word was God." When I pray over you the Word of

God, then I know that I'm actually speaking God talk over your life, and we know that God is not a man that He should lie and that every promise of God is not only yes but amen or so be it as well.

You see my friends, if I speak over your life what I think or feel needs to be prayed, then the question becomes, am I able to accomplish what I'm speaking over your life? The answer is a loud no. Again, the confirmation can be found within the very Word of God where we are told by Jesus Himself in Mark 10:27 "Jesus looked at them and said, "With man this is impossible, but not with God, all things are possible with God." As a matter of fact, this very saying is repeated again in Matthew 19:26 and Luke 18:27.

I can guarantee this truth since I know that with me, it's impossible but with God everything is possible, and I also know that God has given me faith the size of a mustard seed and tells me so in Matthew 17:20 He replied, "Because you have so little faith. Truly, I tell you, if you have faith as small as a mustard seed, you can say to this mountain, 'Move from here to there,', and it will move. Nothing will be impossible for you."

Just to be clear, the bible never told me that I have faith the size of a mustard seed. What it does tell me is for by grace you have been saved through faith. It also says now faith is the assurance of things hoped for, the conviction of things not seen, and I'm also encouraged where I'm told, whatever you ask in prayer; you will receive, if you have faith.

There are few things that I know that I know, and one of them is that I am saved and heaven bound, and that I have faith, and because of my faith, I know that nothing will be impossible for me, especially when I believe that my prayers over you will come to pass because I'm speaking the Word of God or God's word over you.

My responsibility is to pray and believe. Your responsibility is to receive and believe. Interesting, my praying and believing are the same as you're receiving and believing, which boils down to one thing, faith. We are told in Mark 6:5, 6 "And He could do no miracle there except that He laid His hands on a few sick people and healed them. And He wondered at their unbelief. And He was going around the villages teaching."

Was this the same Jesus that we read about in Matthew 9:35 "Jesus went through all the towns and villages, teaching in their synagogues, proclaiming the good news of the kingdom and healing every disease and sickness." You have to agree with me that every sickness, and every disease are a lot of healing.

So what was the problem? Was there an abundance of kryptonite in the home town of Jesus that weakened His power? Of course not, the problem was lack of faith on the ability of He who says nothing is impossible with Me.

If I'm praying and believing, and you're not receiving and believing, don't expect to receive because of your lack of faith and especially because what I'm praying over you is the Word of God, which cannot, has not and will not fail you, not now and not ever.

So my friends, here is my prayer for each of you,

Father, I lift up every single one of my friends and I pray in the name of Jesus, the name which is above every other name that the God and Father of our Lord Jesus Christ, who has blessed you in the Heavenly realms with every spiritual blessing in Christ, and that you would come to that place of knowing that He chose you in him before the creation of the world to be holy and blameless in His sight and that you have been predestined for adoption to Sonship through Jesus Christ, in accordance with His pleasure and will to the praise of His glorious grace, which He has freely given you. I pray that you would come to know that in him, you have redemption through His blood, the forgiveness of sins, in accordance with the riches of God's grace that He lavished on each and every one of you and with all wisdom and understanding, and He continues to make known to you the mystery of His will according to His good pleasure.

I pray that you understand in all wisdom and understanding that when you believed, you were marked in him with a seal, the promised Holy Spirit, who is a deposit guaranteeing your inheritance until the redemption of those who are God's possession, to the praise of His glory.

I continue to keep asking that the God of our Lord Jesus Christ, the glorious Father, may give each of you the Spirit of wisdom and revelation, so that you may know him better. I pray that the eyes of your heart may be enlightened in order that you may know the hope to which He has called you, the riches of His glorious inheritance in His holy people, and His incomparably great power for us who believe. That power is the same as the mighty strength He exerted when He raised Christ from the dead and seated him at His right hand in the Heavenly realms, far above every rule and authority, power and dominion, and every name that is invoked, not only in the present age but also in the one to come.

I pray that you come to comprehend that the fear of the Lord is wisdom, and to depart from evil is understanding and that the LORD, would remember you and take notice of you, and take vengeance on your behalf against your persecutors. I pray my friends that the words of the Lord would be found by you and you would eat them, and the words of the Lord would have become for you, a joy and the delight of your heart, and know that you know you have been called by His name, the LORD the God of Hosts.

My dear friends, I pray that out of His glorious riches, He may strengthen you with power through His Spirit in your inner being, so that Christ may dwell in your hearts through faith. And I pray that you, being rooted and established in love, may have power, together with all the Lord's holy people, to grasp how wide and long and high and deep is the love of Christ, and to know this love that surpasses knowledge—that you may be filled to the measure of all the fullness of God.

I also ask my Heavenly Father that He would help you in your time of weakness, and that you would declare and proclaim boldly that God tells you, fear not, for I am with you, be not dismayed, for I am your God, I will strengthen you; I will help you; I will uphold you with my righteous right hand, so I say to you be strong and courageous. Do not fear or be in dread of the giants in your life, for it is the Lord your God who goes with you. He will not leave you or forsake you. May you know that the Lord also promises you that the Lord will take away from you all sickness, and none of the evil diseases throughout the world, which you knew, will He inflict on you, but He will lay them on all who hate you and when the waves are about to overwhelm you, may your hearts cry be, stand still and see this great thing that the Lord will do before your eyes.

God bless you my friends and truly may the Lord bless you in all of your going out, and coming in, your sitting down, and standing up, may He bless you in your homes, in your family, in your business, and in every area of your life, and may the portals of heaven be opened unto you in every area of your needs from your physical, your medical, your emotional, your financial, and your spiritual, and may God put a hedge of protection around you, and all that belongs to you, and I pray that in the name of Jesus.

Excerpts of this prayer come from the NIV version

Be Careful, For I Am Not As I Was

There's a 2013 movie that I've watched at least a dozen times called The Book of Daniel, by Pure Flix Entertainment, and there's a scene where King Nebuchadnezzar comes to that place where he acknowledges that God is supreme in the affairs of man, and everything that He does is not only right but also just and no one can tell Him no. This recognition comes right after King Nebuchadnezzar had spent the last 7 years wandering about as an animal and eating the food of animals, and because he acknowledges God as the King of Kings, God restores his kingdom, his power and his mind back to him.

In the movie, after being absent from his throne for seven years, the king finally walks back into the throne room fully adorned as king, and all his officials were there, as they were every day for the past seven years which was their duty and their responsibility. One of the officials steps out of line to take a closer look at the king, which would have been punishable by death and King Nebuchadnezzar makes a statement that prompted this message. He says to the official, 'Be careful, for I am not as I was.'

The question becomes, how was he? Well, he was like an animal, eating grass and crawling and wandering about as an animal, cattle to be exact, and now he was once again a king and not just a king, but the most powerful king that the world at that time has ever known. Even today by our standards, the king of Babylon was a powerful ruler over a city that had over 200,000 people.

What really jumped out at me was the comment he made when he said, 'Be careful, for I am not as I was.' As I thought about that statement it became very clear to me that as a believer in Jesus Christ, and growing in the recognition of who we are in Christ, and the authority that we have been given in Christ, and the realization that we are under attack daily from an enemy, that although he can't take away our salvation, he can take away our joy and peace.

How does he take away our peace and joy? We give it to him and allow him to attack us in our weakness because we really don't understand or know who we are in Christ.

We get saved, and are happy with that but don't go after the fullness, and power, and riches that we have in Christ Jesus, as it tells us in 2 Timothy 1:7 "For the Spirit God gave us does not make us timid, but gives us power, love and self-discipline." This is repeated in Ephesians 3:16, "I pray that out of his glorious riches he may strengthen you with power through his Spirit in your inner being,"

Some might be thinking, how do I go after all that God has for me? You do that by studying the Word of God, it was written for you by your loving Father to become all that you could be. According to Philippians 4:8, it tells us "Finally, brothers and sisters, whatever is true, whatever is noble, whatever is right, whatever is pure, whatever is lovely, whatever is admirable, if anything is excellent or praiseworthy, think about such things" and Acts 17:11 "Now the Berean Jews were of more noble character than those in Thessalonica, for they received the message with great eagerness and examined the Scriptures every day to see if what Paul said was true" and Proverbs 18:15 "The heart of the discerning acquires knowledge, for the ears of the wise seek it out."

What do you do with this knowledge? You learn who you are in Christ, and the power, and authority that you have been given in that name which is above all other names. Luke 10:19 "I have given you authority to trample on snakes and scorpions and to overcome all the power of the enemy, nothing will harm you." Did you hear that, we have been given authority which means the right and ability over all the power of the enemy? That word all means entirely, and totally, and completely over the power of the enemy. If we have all authority, then the enemy has none. How come, how can that be? Because we have it all, and it was given to us by Jesus.

As we grow in knowing who we are and the authority and power that we have in Christ the next time the enemy comes to attack us, we can boldly proclaim and tell the enemy the same thing that King Nebuchadnezzar told one of his officials, be careful, for I am not as I was, because the truth is, we are not as we were. Before Jesus, we were dead, but now we are alive, we were living in darkness, and now we have passed into His glorious light. Before Jesus the only thing we could do well was fail, but now we are more than conquerors through him who loved us. We were walking around living a lie, even if we liked it, but now, we know the truth, and the truth has made us free. We were walking in condemnation but now, there is therefore, no condemnation for those who are in Christ Jesus.

Before coming to Jesus, we were the same as every other sinner walking on planet earth, but now we are not as we were. When the enemy comes knocking at your door, you have every right to speak out loud and tell him, be careful for I am not as I was, and you would be absolutely correct.

I'm sure some may be thinking; you mean I'm supposed to actually speak out loud to the enemy? Of course. If Jesus could speak to the wind, and the waves, and to trees, and to demons, then so can we. The enemy can't see into the future and has no idea that you have become such a powerful weapon in the hands of an Almighty God. When the enemy comes to attack you in your weakness or your addiction or in that area which is a stumbling stone, you let him know you are not as you were and declare your victory over those past weaknesses which are now your strengths.

One last thing, when you declare something, you are not declaring what you would like to have but what you possess and own. I'm sure many out there have been to other countries, and when you returned to this country, you always pass through the customs' office, and they have you fill out a declaration form. They don't ask you 'What would you like to have' but 'What do you have in your possession.'

When you make a declaration against the enemy, it's jam-packed with what you have, and what you have are the promises of God, the Word of God and that is more than enough to cause the enemy to flee. Here are a few promises that you can declare, James 4:7 "Submit yourselves therefore to God. Resist the devil, and he will flee from you." Isaiah 54:17 "No weapon forged against you will prevail, and you will refute every tongue that accuses you. This is the heritage of the servants of the LORD, and this is their vindication from me," declares the LORD." John 10:10 "The thief comes only to steal and kill and destroy, I have come that they may have life, and have it to the full."

My friends, the more we get into the Word, the more the word gets into us, and it becomes as a spiritual vitamin which gets deep down, into our spirit and strengthens us from the inside and as that happens, we can declare boldly to the enemy, and any force or power or situation that tries to come against us, be careful, for I am not as I was.

Prayer, Father, thank you that at one time I was in darkness, and now I am in the light. I was dead but now I'm alive, and because of Your great promises for my life, I have been changed, and I am not as I was in the former days.

Children of God Are Resistant

The other day I was walking with Norma, and the Lord dropped a thought in my mind when He said, 'the children of God are resilient.' I knew what resilient meant but had to look it up just to be sure, and it said, resistant, tough, sturdy, and able to bounce back.

The more I thought about this the more I had to agree with what the Lord was saying. It's good to agree with what the Lord says, even if you don't understand what He is saying. He's such a good God that He will explain Himself over and over until you know exactly what He is saying. I wish it were that way with people. Often times I hear words coming out of their mouths but have no idea what they are trying to communicate. About that time, I get the deer in the head light effect.

So God tells me that 'His children are able to bounce back.' Bounce back from what? Truth be told, although we are saved and heaven bound, we still run into rough waters or troubled spots in life, and many times we just get discouraged, annoyed and just plain up-set with what's going on in life. Personally, I've learned that life is a mine field and sometimes when not walking close to the Lord, I step off course and right onto a mine and the whole thing blows up right in my face.

Am I the only one? Of course not, in Psalm 42:6 we are told, "My soul is downcast within me, therefore I will remember you from the land of the Jordan, the heights of Hermon--from Mount Mizar." Again in Lamentations 3:20 "I well remember them, and my soul is downcast within me." Last one, in Psalm 42:5 "Why, my soul, are you downcast? Why so disturbed within me? Put your hope in God, for I will yet praise him, my Savior and my God."

Downcast means depressed, discouraged, sad, disappointed and just plain not right inside. Why would scripture say these things if they weren't a condition of the soul that we all experience?

Jesus himself in Mark 14:36 says, "Abba, Father," he said, "Everything is possible for you. Take this cup from me. Yet not what I will, but what you will." Why would he say that if he wasn't experiencing what it means to be downcast?

I once heard an expression that said 'the difference between a rut and a grave is how long you stay there.' Sometimes things just happen that we never planned on or expected to happen. In Matthew 5:45 it says, "That you may be children of your Father in heaven. He causes his sun to rise upon the evil and the good, and sends rain on the righteous and the unrighteous."

In other words, sometimes good things happen to bad people, and bad things happen to good people. You know sometimes an outdoor wedding gets rained on and the people are really upset, and all their plans are foiled yet that same rain brings joy and thanksgiving to a farmer whose crops desperately needed rain. So who's right in their complaint or thanksgiving to God?

The difference is when things go wrong for an unbeliever, where do they take the complaint? For a child of God, we believe as Jeremiah 33:3 tells us, "Call to me and I will answer you and tell you great and unsearchable things you do not know." It's like the expression I once heard, 'the difference between a believer and a non-believer is when a non-believer calls upon God, and he doesn't get an answer.'

So what does this have to do with being a sturdy people, a people who are tough and resistant? It can all be summed up in Proverbs 24:16 "For though the righteous fall seven times, they rise again, but the wicked stumble when calamity strikes." As children of the Living God, we will bounce back over and over because our eyes are not on the circumstances or the winds or waves of life but upon, He who calms the winds and waves in life.

Prayer, Thank you Lord that I can be called a child of the Living God, and because of Your presence in my life, I can bounce back regardless of the circumstances, because of Your great promises in my life, which are yes and amen.

Expect Delays

As Norma and I were traveling South on a major interstate towards Florida, I noticed numerous signs that displayed their bold message, expect delays. For some reason, these proclamations of what I could expect stuck with me, and I believed that the Lord was prompting me to share with you what He was sharing with me.

Have you ever noticed that we are a society that is not only accustomed to the idea of expecting delays, but that we are confronted with that very reality on a daily basis?

We go into the supermarket, and we expect to be delayed, or we go to any local or federal government building, transportation terminal, any line, anyplace, and we are expected to wait until it's our turn. Even worse, what happens when you've been waiting over an hour in line and just when you get to the front of the line they put up a sign that tells you, see the next window.

It's about that time that we get ready to repent for what we're thinking. I mean, after all what we wanted was to get in and out as quickly as possible. Instead, we are confronted with the very definition of the word delay which is to put off to a later time or cause to be late.

Now my friends, what would you like first, the good news or the bad news?

The bad news, okay, here it is, we can expect delays for the rest of our lives. If we are depending on answers or solutions or advice or any people-oriented services, we can expect delays. We can expect to be held up in lines, buildings, offices, or anywhere we go. Now here's the really frightening reality. Even when we are done waiting, the service or solution or advice may not always be what we were looking for. We came hoping for curtain A, and we ended up with curtain B. In other words; we were disappointed with the outcome. Someone knew what was best for us although what we got wasn't what we wanted or expected.

Here's the good news, In Hebrews 10:37 we are told, "For, "In just a little while, he who is coming will come and will not delay." And again we are encouraged in Revelation 10:6 where we are told, "And he swore by him who lives for ever and ever, who created the heavens and all that is in them, the earth and all that is in it, and the sea and all that is in it, and said, "There will be no more delay!" In other words, when He says that He won't be late, He means it.

The answer may not be according to our timetable, but we can count upon the fact that He will not be early, and He will not be late. When God says He will be doing something in our life, its money in the bank that we can depend on.

So when God speaks to us in Isaiah 43:19 and tells us, "See, I am doing a new thing! Now it springs up, do you not perceive it? I am making a way in the wilderness and streams in the wasteland."

So what did this verse just tell us? God said He will make a way where there is no way, and He will also supply all our needs while we are on the way. God is truly a way maker my friends. He is not a bridge over troubled waters. He makes dry the troubled way and provides a firm, solid path for us to walk upon. The rivers in the wilderness are for our refreshing; they are part of the solution not the problem.

You might be asking yourself the question, how can God do that in my life? I don't see anything new. That's easy my friends, God is God and nothing is too hard for Him, and besides, in Isaiah 42:9 "See, the former things have taken place, and new things I declare, before they spring into being I announce them to you."

You see my friends; God does not speak prophetically; He already knows what is going to happen and spring up in your life. He may use a prophet to speak into your life but that becomes an issue for you of, 'Only believe.'

God is a good God, and wants only the very best in your life, your family, your future, your business, and your walk with Him. He doesn't want you to be filled with doubt or fear, and He certainly doesn't want you to have to wait for His answers to your prayers. The problem my friend is never on God's side of the equation but on our side. We are either way too impatient, or too anxious, or too fearful, or hearing the wrong voices, or we ask God to bless what we are about to do regardless if it came from Him or not because we are looking at a great return from our investment.

Listen to me, the greatest return on your investment is not in the stock market, it's not in the housing industry, not in precious stones or gold. The greatest return on your investment comes about when you invest in the things of God, spend time with Him, in His Word, hear His voice, and seek His advice before you step out and do anything.

When you desire to come into His presence, you will never hear a voice or see a sign telling you to expect delays. You will never get a busy signal, or a detour, or see next window, or the number you have called has been disconnected. Remember when the prayers go up the blessings come down.

God always has time for you and loves walking with you, His child in the cool of the day. He's your Heavenly Dad who is not like a million times better than the best earthly dad; God is totally and completely different than any dad you have ever known, and His love to you goes exceedingly, abundantly beyond anything you can ask or imagine.

Prayer, Father, I know you are my Heavenly Father, but sometimes the detours of life get me to take my eyes off of You, but I ask You to continue to guide me when it's hard for me to see or hear You.

Get Away By Yourself

Interesting, The Lord woke me up at 04:30 so He could meet with me.

I was reading about the Tent of Meeting or the Tabernacle of Meeting also called the Tabernacle of the Congregation in Exodus 33:7 and was amazed that in all reality, it was a portable dwelling place for God's divine presence. What really got my attention was found in verse 9, "Whenever Moses entered the tent, the pillar of cloud would descend and stand at the entrance of the tent, and the LORD would speak with Moses."

As I was reading about this meeting place, I tried to associate or liken it with my own spiritual life, devotion time, and hearing from God.

When reading about people in the bible I would often times sit back and ask myself the question, 'How did these guys actually hear the voice of God?' You know, people like David or Gideon or many of the prophets of old, how did they hear the voice of God. Was it like a big screen in their head or a gut feeling that God was speaking to them or a warm fuzzy they had about making a decision?

One thing for sure, when it came to people like Joshua and having to send an entire army in to battle based on what you thought the voice of God was saying, you better be pretty sure who was speaking or a lot of lives could be lost.

I'm not talking about obedience, I'm talking about hearing. We know their obedience to the plan of God helped them see the victory that they had been promised. Joshua obeyed the command to take the land. He followed God's instructions in crossing the river. He obeyed God's strange plan to defeat the city of Jericho. Though it didn't always make sense, Joshua led the people in obedience to God. As a result, they saw great victories.

I remembered more than once being obedient to what I thought was God's voice only to find out it was my own voice being spiritualized, and not God's voice at all. I'm not speaking about okay God do you want me to buy that big flat screen television, or Lord do you want me to buy those new tools I've been dreaming about, or go on that wonderful cruise for two weeks.

Just recently I had open-heart surgery. More than once I prayed, 'Okay God do you want me to go through with this dangerous surgery or do you want me to trust you for my complete healing as you said in your word.' Was I being serious? You bet, there was no way that I was looking forward to having my chest cracked open, and my heart stopped while the surgeons did what they did best. I was very serious in my praying. Did I hear specifically from the Lord concerning the operation? Not a word, not a yes or no. Was I confused? Of course I was, especially because I hear very clearly from the Lord for other people, and often.

I'm sure there are many of you that have been in the same situation, maybe not the surgery but really needing to hear from God, and not getting anything.

So how does all this tie-in with Exodus 33:7 "It was Moses' practice to take the tent and pitch it outside the camp some distance away, calling it the tent of meeting. Anyone inquiring of the LORD would go to the tent of meeting outside the camp."

First thing I'm going to do is de-construct this verse meaning I'm going to look at it from various perspectives, left to right, and right to left, as-well-as top to bottom, and bottom to top, and with all that I will not add to or subtract from the word of God.

Why would anyone have a need to inquire anything of the Lord? Easy, because you need His direction, and you want to hear His voice on an important matter in your life.

I don't know about you, but I sometimes find it easier to hear the voice of God when I'm alone, and apart from the busy schedules and programs of the rat race that we call progress, and the hectic programs of family life. This may have been a reason why the meeting place of God was pitched outside the camp some distance away. It's always a good idea to have a quiet place where you can meet with God, and not have all the distractions, and clutter that are associated with life.

Another thing I noticed about getting alone with God was, it was Moses' practice. You see; it was his normal way of meeting with God, in other words, this preparation to meet with God was a recurrence in his life. Not that it was a dull, ordinary, mundane, same ole, same ole, but it was an exciting life changing event that he was looking forward to. Moses wasn't meeting with his working buddy; he was meeting with God, and he was accustomed to getting results from his meeting.

How do I know that Moses got results? Because Exodus 33:9 tells us, "When Moses entered the tent, the pillar of cloud would come down and stand at the doorway of the tent while God spoke with Moses."

This isn't a case of someone saying, 'I spoke with God today', oh really? Look at verse 10, "Whenever the people saw the pillar of cloud standing at the entrance to the tent, they all stood and worshiped, each at the entrance to their tent." That tells me that the presence of God was evident with physical manifestations that everyone could see.

Moses or anyone needing to inquire of the Lord would get alone to a quiet place away from the hustle and bustle of life, and there they would meet with God, and it was there that they would get results because God still desires to meet with His children, and that includes you my friends. If it wasn't so, why would we be told in Psalm 59:10 "My God on whom I can rely." God will go before me and will let me gloat over those who slander me.

Not only is getting alone with God a great idea but it was the very heart of Jesus himself.

Mark 1:35 "Very early in the morning, while it was still dark, Jesus got up, left the house and went off to a solitary place, where he prayed."

Matthew 14:23 "After he had dismissed them, he went up on a mountainside by himself to pray. When evening came, he was there alone."

Luke 6:12 "One of those days Jesus went out to a mountainside to pray, and spent the night praying to God."

Think about this my friends, investing your time alone with God will have the best return from your investment.

Prayer, Lord, It seems with the hectic, busy schedules of life, that getting alone with you isn't as easy as I thought it would be. Help me to set my priorities and focus upon the things that are truly important in life, and that means putting You first in all that I say and do.

Give Me a Break

It's absolutely amazing how God can speak to us in any situation using anything that He wants to get His message across, and His messages can really change your life forever.

A number of weeks ago Norma and I were staying with some friends in Georgia; something happened that I really would like to share with you.

These friends subscribe to a medical journal, and as I was walking into the kitchen the Lord spoke to me, as only He can speak, and said, 'Look at the magazine on the table." So being the obedient person that I am, at least in this one case, I glanced down to see the title of the main article which read, 'Looking for the Heart that Cares.' Obviously it had something to do with a cardiovascular issue but the title jumped off the magazine and spoke to my Spirit. Thank you Lord.

I began to think about society in general, and many of my friends hurts and needs that exist in their lives, and in our world.

I realized that people are looking for a heart that cares. I think you'll agree that people need to know they matter, and that there's someone out there that unconditionally loves them in spite of their faults. You know what I mean, someone that we can be real not ideal or plastic with.

Someone whom we don't have to perform for to get attention or acceptance. In other words, that someone who loves us for who we are, not what we can do or what they get from us.

Sometimes it seems that everyone wants a piece of the action. The government, the IRS, school, teachers, friends, family, and the list just goes on and on. No wonder at the end of the day, we are so exhausted, and it's not only from work. There are pressures without and pressures within that all have a tendency to work on our emotional state and wear us down.

Often times we just get tired of performing for others, regardless of who they are. That's probably why we look forward to the weekend or a vacation or just being alone, and when I say alone, I mean alone without our mind beating us up or reminding us of what we so desperately need to forget. That's why sometimes we yell and tell others, 'I Need Some Rest.'

David says exactly the same thing when he said, "Answer me when I call to you, O God who declares me innocent. Free me from my troubles. Have mercy on me and hear my prayer," Psalms 4:1. In other words, give me relief from my distress, I need some rest.

Well, I have great news, there is a place of rest, and there is someone who loves us unconditionally, and there is a heart that cares so much that He provides us with the very thing that we so desperately need.

I know you know the scripture, but you and I need to know that we really know who this person is, and where that rest is. Head knowledge really doesn't seem to cut it when we are confronted with life-size issues and troubles.

I know my medication will help me, but if I don't use it, what's the point in knowing that it will help me? Knowing there's a place of rest doesn't help me, unless I go there to rest. Knowing that someone loves me unconditionally doesn't do me any good if I continue to act and perform to get His acceptance and love. That's not rest, that's work.

Jesus tells us in Matthew 11:28 "Come to me, all you who are weary and burdened, and I will give you rest." One thing I know is that a person can't give what they don't have, yet here Jesus says He will give us rest.

In Hebrews 4:1 it tells us, "Therefore, since the promise of entering his rest still stands, let us be careful that none of you be found to have fallen short of it." And in Hebrews 4:9, it takes it a step further and says, "There remains, then, a Sabbath-rest for the people of God."

That's pretty comforting to know that Jesus gives us that rest, and His promise for that rest still stands, and that rest period really does exist.

I guess the problem with rest is in the definition that we give to rest.

Bing says rest is, Cessation of work, exertion, or activity, it also tells us, it's, Peace, ease, or refreshment resulting from sleep or the cessation of an activity.

In the Greek, rest is to be exempt or to have an intermission.

We sometimes define a rest as a few minutes break in a fast paced, hectic race through the day.

Some years ago, a Tacoma, Washington's newspaper ran a story about Tattoo, an eight-month-old basset hound who went for an unplanned run one day. When his owner

54

accidentally shut the dog's leash in the car door and took off for a drive, Tattoo had no choice but to try to keep up. Fortunately, a motorcycle officer saw the passing vehicle with something being dragged behind it. However, before Tattoo's owner finally stopped, and the dog was rescued; the vehicle had reached speeds of up to 25 miles per hour. Although Tattoo was dragged some of the way, he was not injured. Imagine poor Tattoo with his little basset hound legs, trying to keep up.

We need a time out from the rat race, and so I have good news for you.

Jesus gives us rest; His promise for that rest still stands, and that rest period really does exist. Let's take advantage of it and take time to smell the roses.

Prayer, Heavenly Father, I know all Your promises are yes and amen, and that You have given me a place of rest. Help me to make the time, and to take the time to enter into that rest, and just sit by Your feet and learn from You.

God, Can You Wait a Second?

God, can You wait a second? Can you imagine actually saying that to God, and I don't mean in prayer; I mean while He is standing right in front of you, big as life? Who would have the nerve to do something like that? Well, some pretty big hitters in the Old Testament.

It Judges 6:18 "Please do not go away until I come back and bring my offering and set it before you." And the LORD said, "I will wait until you return."

This is very similar to Genesis 18:5 "Let me get you something to eat, so you can be refreshed and then go on your way--now that you have come to your servant." "Very well," they answered, "do as you say."

I find that absolutely amazing, Gideon prepared a goat and Abraham prepared a calf. To prepare a goat in a pot has to take at least an hour and 45 minutes just for the cooking time, and another 40 minutes for the preparation of the animal. For a calf, this animal weighs about 150 pounds so it probably took a lot longer to get this ready for consumption.

Obviously, this teaching is not going to be about meat products but something far more interesting and really quite amazing.

In both cases, Gideon and Abraham are speaking to God, and they say to God, and I'm paraphrasing the situation, but it boils down to, 'God, can you wait a second while I go to make lunch for you'. If that isn't amazing in itself, how about this, God says 'Yes, I'll wait right here for you, I won't go away, go and do what you said.'

This isn't like going to the freezer, and taking out some frozen chicken or a frozen steak. This is getting the live animal, and starting from scratch; it was a big deal. I mean, there were times I cooked for guests and got started a little late while company waited, and I know how uncomfortable I felt while dinner cooked, and they entertained themselves in the living room with TV or whatever. Again, I mean it wasn't like God was in the living room of the tent watching a football game. God was waiting, and it would be at least two hours for everything to be cooked and served. No pressure right?

Now I know that God is love, and compassionate, and faithful, but we're talking about patience. Why would God be so patient with Gideon, Abraham and us? I know that 2 Peter 3:15 tells us "Bear in mind that our Lord's patience means salvation." But why would God wait hours while a meal was being prepared?

The key is to be found in the word 'Offering' that Gideon used before God. Offering in Hebrew is the word "minchah" pronounced min-khaw, and actually means a present but more than that, it means a sacrificial, voluntary gift or tribute. What was Gideon going to do with this tribute? He was going to lay it before God. That word 'Lay' is Qal and means to rest or settle down, and remain, or to be quiet or cease from any activity.

So why would God be patient enough to wait for Gideon? Because Gideon was a person that used expressions that we use all the time, Is that really you God? If that's really you God show me. If you do this, I might believe, if you do that I might believe, are you talking to me God? These expressions came from Gideon's heart, and there had to be a closure to the doubts inside before there could be victories on the outside.

Gideon's present was more than a lunch; it was himself, and his doubts of who he was and who God is, and what God can do with an available person. Gideon's sacrifice was to present his doubts once and for all to God and lay his restlessness at God's feet and cease from all activities, especially the ones that caused him to question God's power to make Gideon more than he could be by himself.

So what did Gideon say? 'God, can you wait here while I go and prepare my heart from the inner battles of who I am and who You are and lay them at Your feet and leave them at your feet as I submit myself to Your Lordship?'

Will God be patient and wait while you bring your doubts and insecurities and concerns to Him? You bet. God will wait as long as it takes to bring you to a place of total assurance of who He is, and who you can become in Him. Truly, 2 Peter 3:15 is very accurate as it reveals to us that the Lord's patience means salvation. Who's salvation? Our salvation. And what is salvation if it isn't God's divine passion and love for His children and reveals God's safeguarding which is deliverance from destruction, difficulty, or evil for His children.

Prayer, Lord, Help me to stop walking away from Your presence and to finally, lay down my heart, my desires and my needs and to just wait on You to help me become all that You have destined me to become. Thank you Lord for your patience, and great love that You have for me.

Have you Considered My Servant?

The other day I was conducting a bible study, and a precious saint asked me a question. What do you do when you are serving the Lord the best way you know how, spending time in the word, and time with the Lord, and it seems that God is so far away from you and the only company you have is a dark cloud that seems to be following you wherever you go, and the blessings of God are seemingly so far away? What do you do, was the main question?

It reminded me so very much of the story in Job where it tells us of Job's good life and starts in Job 1:1 "There was a man in the land of Uz whose name was Job. And that man was pure and upright, one who feared God and turned away from evil." In Job 1:8 it seems the dark cloud was given permission to follow Job wherever he went as we are told, "So the Lord said to Satan, "Have you considered my servant Job? There is no one like him on the earth, a pure and upright man, one who fears God and turns away from evil."

Granted it was an opportunity to look at Job's integrity in the midst of adversity. Ultimately, the question has to be asked, what was the purpose of the adversity? Was it for God's sake? The Lord already knew Job was a pure and upright man, one who feared God and turned away from evil, He even mentioned it twice. Was it for Satan's sake?

Who really cares what Satan thinks seeing that he will twist everything around regardless of what truth is spoken. Who's left, Job? Was it for Job's sake that the adversity was turned loose on him and his family? I mean if the reward for being a person of integrity and morality, and a follower of God, and one who turns away from evil and you are rewarded with what Job received, you might want to re-consider your position. I mean after all, if losing your entire family, all your sons and daughters were a way to make a point, thank you, but no thank you might be a statement for one who doesn't understand the story behind Job, and the actions of the main players of the story.

So let's take a closer look at the players. In no particular order, there is God, Job, and Satan, and if you have ever read the story or heard about Job, then the audience is a player in this story, that means you the reader of the story.

Job 1:22 tells us, "In all this Job did not sin, nor did he charge God with moral impropriety which means, bad behavior or bad choice." In other words, God how could you let this happen to me? I mean, after all I've done, and doing for You. God, this is not your best decision, and I'm sure there are dozens of people out there much more worthy to suffer than me and my family, as a matter of fact; I have a list of names that You might want to consider. I mean with friends like you who needs enemies.

I think you'll agree with me that grief can have you making statements that you will repent for later in your walk with God. But as I'm so fond of saying, 'God can handle your honesty much more than your hypocrisy.' Meaning, your honesty will not cause God to be shocked where He will close up shop and go in to another line of business, after all, we are told that He knows the ending from the beginning, in Isaiah 41:4 "I, the Lord, am present at the very beginning, and at the very end – I am the one." You see; Job like the rest of us cannot understand what the adversity in our lives has to do with our Godly walk. However, in Ecclesiastes 3:11 it states, "God has made everything fit beautifully in its appropriate time, but he has also placed ignorance in the human heart so that people cannot discover what God has ordained, from the beginning to the end of their lives."

We all, like Job, have situations in our lives that we would rather not have to go through. Even so, all the situations in our lives will either be a building stone or a stumbling stone.

The question should not be why me Lord, but how will this draw me closer to you Lord?

One thing I have personally learned, is that pain hurts, and I don't like it. That doesn't mean that I won't experience it again, and I don't have to like it, but it will do one of two things in my life. It will either draw me closer to the Lord or cause me to run from the Lord.

The next player in this story is God, and since His ways are so much higher than my ways, I am reminded over and over again that I can never understand God's ways, and I really don't want to think that I can, I'm going to play it safe and say 'God you know.'

I will discuss the next player who is Satan, and I won't spend a lot of time on him. Job's life is an example of a committed believer in God and all the adversity that may come along will not shake the faith of a believer. Like Job 1:21 we proclaim and declare with boldness, "Naked I came from my mother's womb, and naked I will return there. The Lord gives, and the Lord takes away. May the name of the Lord be blessed?" In other words, I didn't have anything when I came into this world and everything I have from worldly possessions to family and friends are a gift from God, my Heavenly Father, and if He chooses to remove any or all of them, it's His choice and I will trust Him regardless of what may happen, after all, they were never mine to start with but were on loan from He who is the giver of all good gifts.

You see with the integrity of that kind of a person; God can with all assurances say to the enemy, 'Have you considered My servant? Regardless of what I allow you to do to him, this servant will not waver in his faith, nor will he turn away from Me. As a matter of fact Satan, the more you throw at him the closer he will draw unto Me. He will draw so close to Me, that I will be in him and he will be in Me, but this is something you don't understand and can never understand, it's called the love of the Father to the children of God.'

And finally, the audience, that's you and me, the last players in this story. What does this story reveal to us? It shows us that regardless of the situations that may come upon us; we can and will be strong. We can either put our eyes on the winds and waves or on the one who calms the winds and waves in our lives. It shows us that God truly is faithful to a thousand generations and that He and only He has our lives in His hands, and that the enemy doesn't have the right or permission to do with us what he wants to do. If it were up to the enemy, he would want to destroy us immediately because he doesn't like the Christ centered, God-fearing saints of God. As it says in 1 Peter 5:8 "Be sober and alert. Your enemy the devil, like a roaring lion, is on the prowl looking for someone to devour and that means to consume or dispose of." It's hard to devour someone who is under the hedge of God's protection without the permission of God himself.

As we look at the unfolding story of Job, we can sympathize with Job's loss but we can also be encouraged with God's faithfulness in his life knowing that we are never forsaken or abandoned by our Heavenly Father. As in the case of Job, when it seems that God is so far from us, it's really a chance for God to enter a personal dialogue directly with us. As is the case in Job 38:1 "Then the LORD spoke to Job from out of the whirlwind."

Did anything change in Job's life prior to God speaking to him? No, absolutely nothing, he still lost his family, but when God enters the scene everything changes because you can't come into the presence of God and leave exactly the same way you came in. God makes the difference.

So my friends be encouraged, you might be going through a season right now that is as black as a moonless night, but it will only be for a season, and joy will once again come in the morning, and God is only a prayer away.

Prayer, Father, sometimes when the winds and the waves of my life seem to be more then I can bear, I know that You are just a prayer away, and You always come to my aid in times of trouble. Help me to rely on you and on You only for my deliverance.

God Where Are You?

Have you ever asked yourself the question, 'Who or what or where is God?' The good news is, the very answer to those questions can be found in the very Word of God.

God's Word version says, "The name of the LORD is a strong tower. A righteous person runs to it and is safe."

The Amplified version says, "The name of the Lord is a strong tower, the consistently righteous man upright and in right standing with God runs into it and is safe, high above evil and strong."

Throughout Scripture, names were always important. Names often stood for the character of the one they represented. When a person's life changed direction, often they received a new name. For example, Abraham, Jacob, and Paul were given new names and a new direction in life.

The name of God means more than a proper name or label for God. A person's name especially that of a king or ruler, stood for the authority of that person. This is same notion in the Great Commission when Jesus tells his disciples to baptize new disciples 'In the name of the Father, Son, and Holy Spirit.' The term, 'name' stands for more than just a word. Behind it lies all the honor, glory, and dominion of God.

Over and over, scripture makes a comparison of the Lord to a strong tower or a refuge or a fortress.

One thing we need to be aware of is the fact that ancient readers could easily understand the value of a strong tower. Present day readers would not comprehend the picture quite as eagerly, which is why scripture should always be interpreted in its cultural and ancient setting. The image of a strong tower indicates that God is our secure refuge or protection or shelter.

For example, Psalm 18:2 states, "The LORD is my rock, my fortress and my deliverer, my God is my rock, in whom I take refuge. He is my shield and the horn of my salvation, my stronghold." Again in Proverbs 14:26, "He who fears the LORD has a secure fortress, and for his children it will be a refuge."

Interesting, it tells us the name of the Lord is a strong tower. It doesn't say the Lord is a strong tower, just the name of the Lord. It's indicating that the very name of God has a defending and safe characteristic about it.

The name of the Lord is the same as the presence of the Lord, so where His word is there He is.

When we come right down to it, we find that the source of the security of the believer lies in the character of God and only the character of God.

I know some might be thinking; it's the covenant, but what is the covenant worth, if God were unpredictable, unjust and untruthful?

Why are we actually in need of a fortress or a high tower to run to?

We need a Mighty Fortress because we are constantly being attacked. We need a Mighty Fortress because we need protection, and with God as our Mighty Fortress, we will not fear.

As mentioned, names are very important. Our name can make up our character and the outcome of events in our lives. This might sound strange, but it's true. Names mean a lot, and it could be for good or evil.

Example, Abraham was first called Abram but God said to him that He had made him a father of many nations, and He changed his name to Abraham, which meant father of many nations. Every time Abraham spoke his name or someone else did; the promise of God drew closer. Today Abraham is the father of many nations just as God promised. Another name is that of Jabez one who had his unhappy name blessed. His name meant pain. He didn't want to cause pain, so he prayed and God answered his prayer.

To have a secure fortress means all areas of you are protected and safe, so the question becomes where exactly is God in relation to where I am? Sometimes while being attacked, we feel that God is distant from us, or we feel that we are in this battle alone. How many times have we asked or thought, 'Where are You in all this mess?' Well my friends, let me give you some good news,

He is above me. Deuteronomy 4:39 "Acknowledge and take to heart this day that the LORD is God in heaven above and on the earth below. There is no other."

He is underneath me. Deuteronomy 33:27 "The eternal God is your refuge, and underneath are the everlasting arms. He will drive out your enemies before you, saying, 'Destroy them!'"

God's behind me. Psalm 139:5 "You hem me in behind and before, and you lay your hand upon me."

God's before me. Psalm 16:8 "I have set the LORD always before me, because he is at my right hand, I shall not be shaken.

God's at my right hand. Psalm 110:5 "The Lord is at your right hand, he will crush kings on the day of his wrath."

God's round about me. Psalm 125:2 "As the mountains are round about Jerusalem, so the LORD is round about his people from henceforth even forever."

God's within me. Galatians 2:20 "I have been crucified with Christ and I no longer live, but Christ lives in me. The life I now live in the body, I live by faith in the Son of God, who loved me and gave himself for me."

So my friends, Where is God? He's all around you, all you have to do is call out to Him and He's there as a strong tower for your protection.

Prayer, Father, Sometimes I lose sight of where You are and who You are, especially when things are not going the way I planned for things to go in my life. Help me to always be aware of Your presence, and to call out for You to intervene in my life.

He Has Heard My Cry for Mercy

Thank God we serve a God that hears our cry for mercy and exhibits divine intervention. I'm working on this message from 38,000 feet as we head to London, and on to Germany. As many know, I'm not fond of flying, and when The Lord said low, I will be with you, I figure He meant low, like close to the ground. As a result, I cry for mercy as we jet across the Atlantic Ocean on our way to a Christ filled, God centered journey of a lifetime.

There is nothing more heart breaking than crying out and thinking or believing our cries are falling on deaf ears. The very reason we are crying out is we have come to a place, like many have come to, and that's where we can no longer carry the burden within our heart, and we have no place to turn. We've tried sharing with friends and family, and it sometimes seems they just don't understand. We've tried opening our heart to our spouse, and for some reason, they don't seem to get it, and we often times feel we are all alone with the issue we are going through in our mind. However, here in Psalm 28:6 we are told that when nothing else works, we turn, as a last resort and cry out or pour out our heart to The Lord, and He has all the time to hear our dilemma or problems.

In Proverbs 15:29, "The LORD is far from the wicked, but he hears the prayer of the righteous." In other words, He hears the cry of His children. Again in Psalm 34:15 "The eyes of the LORD are on the righteous, and his ears are attentive to their cry,"

Godly? I don't feel godly. My friends, we are Godly and righteous not because of what we do, or how we act, but because He calls us Godly and righteous, and because of His Son. We were adopted into a Godly and righteous family, and as sons and daughters, we now have the right and privilege of being called Godly and righteous.

I remembered many years ago going through a situation in my life, and it seemed that no one understood what I was going through, and even worse, few wanted to take the time to even discuss it with me. Talk about being out there in left field all alone. I was in a desperate, shaky place during my life, and when everything else failed, I tried to cry out to The Lord. My situation wasn't picture perfect at that season of my life, and I wasn't even sure if The Lord heard me or wanted to hear me. I knew what scripture said, but based on my life's situation, if I was The Lord, I wouldn't listen to my cry. Thank God He's on the throne and not me.

Anyway, I laid my heart before Him, and He heard me. I knew in the deepest place of my inner being that He heard me. I didn't need any proof or any signs from heaven; I just knew. As a result, I experienced the peace that exceeds all understanding as we are told in Philippians 4:7 "And the peace of God, which transcends all understanding, will guard your hearts and your minds in Christ Jesus."

As I walked through the lion's den of my life in that situation, I also experienced the Peace of God, and I knew He was guarding my heart and mind. How did I know? Because I felt His presence, and knew He was in control of this situation. That's why I'm fond of saying that He is in control of my out of controls.

What was my heart cry at that moment? The same as what the Psalmist tells us, "Praise be to the Lord, for he has heard my cry for mercy." He and only He understood what I was going through, and what I was feeling. My cries weren't falling on deaf ears, and even more rewarding was the fact that He actually wanted to hear what it was that was taking away my joy and my peace, and He was willing and able to turn my mourning into joy, meaning; He can take my worst-case situation, and turn it into a major victory in my life. With the Lord, it's never an out of sight, out of mind experience. How could it be when He Himself says in Matthew 28:20 "And surely I am with you always, to the very end of the age."

Many of you know what I'm speaking about. We have all been in situations where the doctors said there was no hope, or the bank said the payments were due soon, or your life seemed to be going nowhere, and He heard your cry for mercy and turned the entire situation around. Much like what happened to Mordecai in Esther 7:9 it says, "Harbona, one of the eunuchs present with the king, said, "What a coincidence! The 75-foot gallows Haman made to hang Mordecai on who by the way spoke up for the well-being of the king is still standing at Haman's house." The king responded, "Hang Haman on it!" Again in Esther 8:2 we read, "The king took off his signet ring which he had taken from Haman, and gave it to Mordecai." By the way, the signet ring represented the power and authority from the king. It's that type of a situation, one moment they want to hang you, and the next moment you are promoted to a position much greater than where you were. One moment the doctors say there's no hope, the next moment they tell you they can't find anything wrong with you. You have a week to find a place to live, and you go to the Lord saying you need a one bedroom apartment for so much per month,

71

and He opens doors for an entire furnished home for half the price. You see only God opens a door that we need to step into because it could have only come from His provision.

Your stumbling stone became your building stone. Your wilderness experience has provided you with valuable firsthand knowledge of God's faithfulness, and the level of intimacy that He desires to have with us. Isn't it ironic that many times it almost seems that He is the one who initiates first contact, and the shakiest times throughout our lives become the most treasured experiences that originate out of the Father's heart towards His children?

Prayer, Father, I know that I don't have because I don't ask. Help me to look to You first when situations seem to be out of control and when I do ask, to have a heart of expectation, and to wait for the answer.

How Great Is My God

Today's sharing is going to be about one thing, and only one thing, namely, how great is our God.

I can't imagine how many times we've sung songs about how great is our God, or shared with others about how great is The Lord. If you're anything like me, it's probably daily, even if it means telling myself that my God is great.

When speaking about our great God it often times revolved around statements like God's mighty power, or His faithfulness to a thousand generations, or His love, and mercy, and compassion.

I thought to myself, 'God has to be much more than that,' so I decided to study the book of Job to find other examples of how great and mighty our God is.

I was convinced that all we see, or hear, or smell, or touch concerning God's greatness was only touching the fringe of His ways. The word fringe means outlying, which means just touching a tangent of God's greatness.

Let me put it this way for the visual among us. Imagine a circle of 360 degrees, and each degree represents just a single dot. A tangent to the circle is where a single line comes into contact with a single dot. Now imagine that God is the circle and everything we know of Him is just a single dot. That means there are 359 other dots that go beyond the realm of our understanding. This is why I'm fond of telling people, everything we have God gave us, but don't think for a moment that He gave us everything that He has.

We serve a great and mighty God. How great and mighty you might be asking? Well, I'm glad you asked because according to the book of Job, our God is so big that: the ghosts and their neighbors in the underworld shake with fear, and death is not hidden from our God.

Did you know that God stretched the northern sky over empty space and hung the earth on nothing? Just an FYI, not too long ago scientists directed the largest telescope towards the northern sky, and they found nothing. There were no stars in that part of the heavens, there was nothing, just like God said in His word.

So how great is our God? Our God drew the horizon on the ocean like a circle where light and darkness meet. He is so mighty that when He threatens the very foundations that hold up the sky, they shake with fear, and the breath of our God makes the skies clear.

How about this, our God is so great that wisdom is hidden from every living thing on earth, birds can't see it, death and destruction say they have never seen it but only heard rumors about it, and only God knows the way to wisdom and knows where it is. Not only that, God has examined and determined the very worth of wisdom. Wow!

Our God sees everything under the sky, and gives wind its power and determines how big the oceans will be, and where the rain and thunderstorms are to go. Imagine that, rain and thunderstorms just don't happen, they are told when and where to happen and when to stop.

You see my friends; these are things that Job and his friends had to say about the greatness of God, but this is what God has to say about Himself,

He made the earth and decided how big it should be. God even measured it with a measuring line, and put the first stone on earth in its place. Our God set the limits for the seas and put it behind locked gates so it can come so far but not an inch further with its great waves.

Our God commands the morning when to begin and when too end and when to shine upon the earth. Our God has walked on the deepest part of the ocean floors like you and I walk in the park. Our God knows exactly where the gates to the world of the dead are, that dark place of death.

Our God knows where light and darkness come from and can take them back to where they belong, and they have to obey Him. Our God knows exactly where the storerooms of snow and hail are, and He keeps them there for times of trouble or war or battle.

Our God is so great that He digs ditches in the sky for heavy rain and makes paths for thunderstorms. Our God is so great that when we look up into the night sky at the constellation Orion and its belt, God says He can unfasten that belt even though it's made up of very large stars. And speaking of stars, God says He put each and every one exactly where they are and controls the laws that control the sky.

Our God says He shouts at the clouds and commands them to cover us with rain. God even tips them over to pour out their rain. He commands lightning and they respond to Him by saying 'Here we are, what do you want sir?' and then go where God tells them to go.

These are just a few of the things that our great and mighty God says He does. And these are in the natural scientific realm of things. What our God does for animals is absolutely amazing. Here are just a few things that God says He does; our God gives the horse its strength, puts the mane on its neck and makes it able to jump like a locust. God taught the hawk how to spread its wings and fly south and told the eagle to fly high in the sky and where to build its nests among the mountains.

God knows where all the mountain goats are born, and watches when the mother deer gives birth. God gave the wild donkeys the desert for a home, and the salt lands for them to live in. God tells us that even wild bulls agree to serve Him.

So my friends, having said all that, I believe we can all agree that we really do serve an awesome God and with Him absolutely, nothing is impossible.

Prayer, Almighty God, It's true that my eye has not seen or my ear hear the greatness of who You are. Help me to realize that with all that power, and might, that you are still my Father, and I am Your child.

I Am Your Shelter and Protection

I'd like to share with you from Nahum 1:7 which declares, "The LORD is good, a refuge in times of trouble. He cares for those who trust in him," the NLV says it this way, "The LORD is good, a stronghold in the day of trouble, And He knows those who take refuge in Him."

This verse brought me back to an incident that happened when we were still living in Chesapeake, Virginia. There was hurricane that was heading our way, Norma and I decided our home might not stand the 90 plus mile per hour winds that were already being recorded, and there were other winds predicted at 120 mph.

We contacted our good friends who lived in Suffolk, and asked if they would mind if we weathered out the storm in their home. Their home is one of those huge homes built around the turn of the century with 30-foot ceilings. They said sure, come on over, and we did, as quickly as we could.

You see, what was bearing down on us was a day of trouble or troubled times, and what was needed was a refuge or a stronghold, and this home with its thick concrete walls was as close to that as we could find. Anyway, the storm hit with all its strength as predicted. In our Chesapeake home, it would have been a fearful thing, even while trusting in the Lord. I realized that wisdom and trust go hand-in-hand

We sat in a sheltered room in this home, and with our eyes, we watched as large trees were up-rooted and knocked over. We witnessed 90 mph winds whipping by us with such force that the sound was like a train. Branches, pieces of homes and all types of debris were flying all around us, but we were secure, and totally safe in this stronghold. As a matter-of-fact, we were even able to drink coffee in the midst of the storm.

Here in Nahum 1:7 "It says that "The LORD is good, a stronghold in the day of trouble, and He knows those who take refuge in Him." In other words, the Lord knows there will be times of trouble, there will be times of problems in your life, there will be challenges, situations and events that you cannot handle in your own strength. In many cases when we try to deal with the situations we only make matters worse causing us to become even more frantic.

I know you trust in the Lord, and are saved, and heaven bound but trust me, there will be troubles in your life. This is not a negative confession but telling you what the Word of God is telling you. In Jeremiah 17:17 states, "Do not be a terror to me, you are my refuge in the day of disaster." Again in Psalm 37:39 "The salvation of the righteous comes from the LORD, he is their stronghold in time of trouble." In Joel 3:16 "The LORD will roar from Zion and thunder from Jerusalem, the earth and the heavens will tremble. But the LORD will be a refuge for his people, a stronghold for the people of Israel."

These are amazing promises. "The earth and the heavens will tremble, just like during the hurricane that struck us many years ago, but the Lord will be a refuge for his people, like that secure, strong home was a refuge for us who waited out the storm in an atmosphere of total and complete security.

There are a few things that I know that I know, and one of them is we will each experience troubled times that are different from each other. For some, it might be financial hard times, for others it could be medical situations, and for others it might be a family disaster. The situations will change and be different, but our refuge will be one and the same because the Lord is our stronghold and our refuge.

In Psalm 46:1 each and every one of us is encouraged with "God is our refuge and strength, an ever-present help in trouble." In other words, God is our refuge and strength, always ready to help us in times of trouble.

I don't know what your time of trouble will look like, but I do know that God will be your refuge and strength, He will be your ever-present help during that time of trouble, and He is always ready to help us when we need Him the most.

What exactly is a refuge? It's a shelter or protection from danger or distress; it's a place or state of safety. Even in Hebrew refuge means a place of shelter, and hope, and listen to this, it also means a place of trust from falsehood.

My friends, that's our God. In times of trouble not only will He protect us physically but will also place us in a shelter, and guard us emotionally and mentally so the enemy will not come in with his lies when we are in a very vulnerable place, and apt to believe the enemies lie like when the doctors tell us there's nothing more to do, go get your things in order or right now there are no jobs out there, and you won't be able to take care of your family. God says 'I will be your shelter and protection; I will be the strength that you need right now since you have very little of your own, I will be all that you need to make it through these troubled times.'

Prayer, Gracious, Heavenly Father, I know that challenging times will be in my life, and that there will be reports that I don't want to hear, but help me to be glad that all of Your promises are yes and amen, and help me to trust in You.

I Don't Like Waiting

I'd like to share with you something that we need to reflect upon as we go through our daily routine of life, and in many cases, which will involve waiting for a thing or many things to happen. The question becomes, what do we do with that which we called waiting?

If you're like me, I really don't like waiting, and I really, don't like waiting for something that is important to me. And I really, really don't like waiting for something that was my mistake the first time, and now I have to wait to do it over. It's like the expression, 'You don't have time to do it right the first time, but you always seem to have time to do it right the second time.'

The other day Norma asked me 'What am I going to do while I'm waiting on the Lord?' I responded by saying 'Why do I have to do anything, why can't waiting on Him be enough?'

It would seem that we are a society of always waiting for one thing or another. We wait to grow up; we wait for our children to grow up; we wait to get a job, or we wait to get married. Truly, we are people that are always waiting for something. Often times when we get what we were waiting for, we're disappointed because it wasn't exactly what we had in mind. It's like what Sharon Creech said in her article, Absolutely Normal Chaos, 'Then I thought, boy, isn't that just typical? You wait and wait and wait for something, and then when it happens, you feel sad.'

What is it exactly that we don't like about waiting? I guess it's that waiting just takes so long, and we forget the purpose of waiting. We see waiting often times as a negative thing, and not a process in itself. John Ortberg said, 'Biblically, waiting is not just something we have to do until we get what we want. Waiting is part of the process of becoming what God wants us to be.' How true, and you know my friends, when we don't see it that way, we become as T.D. Jakes put it 'Spiritually spastic, trying to make the right things happen at the wrong time.'

Why is it? We have such a hard time waiting, and when it takes a little longer than expected, we feel the need to help the process along by doing something, anything just to be useful so as to shorten the process of waiting. I've also discovered that waiting without patience can be very painful, and makes the time take so much longer.

As Fulton J. Sheen said, 'Patience is power. Patience is not an absence of action, rather it is timing, it waits on the right time to act, for the right principles and in the right way.'

Waiting often times is much more rewarding then the actual getting of what we were waiting for. Example, in scripture there are many verses that deal with waiting, and although the reward is great, what we learned in the process is so much greater.

For example, Isaiah 40:30-33 "Even youths shall faint and be weary, and young men shall fall exhausted, but they who wait for the LORD shall renew their strength, they shall mount up with wings like eagles, they shall run and not be weary, they shall walk and not faint."

Here we are told 'That those who wait shall mount up with the wings like eagles and those that wait will be able to run and not become tired, and they can walk and not faint.' Why, because the object of their waiting is not on things or people but upon the Lord.

This is confirmed again in Psalm 37:9 "For those who are evil will be destroyed, but those who hope in the LORD will inherit the land." Imagine, those who are waiting on the Lord will inherit the land but the evil doers in their lives will be cut off.

J.J. Packer in 'Knowing God' tells us, "Wait on the Lord' is a constant refrain in the Psalms, and it is a necessary word, for God often keeps us waiting. He is not in such a hurry as we are, and it is not his way to give more light on the future than we need for action in the present, or to guide us more than one step at a time." When in doubt do nothing, but continue to wait on God. When action is needed light will come. Sometimes this light comes as being able to run or walk or having one's enemies cut off or being able to mount up as an eagle. In other words, waiting has a definite purpose, and a very real return on its investment.

It's how and what we do during the waiting that's important, and by the way, while it's not wrong to complain to God, it is wrong to complain about God during your waiting season.

Besides, there's really not much you can do when waiting is the only option you have. You can either wait and trust in God or wait and depend upon your own understanding, or your intellect, or wealth, but waiting has no respect for the things of man because waiting is a process with a definite ending which is much greater than the object of your waiting.

Have you ever noticed that when you complain during the waiting process, it always seems to take longer? It's like the saying, 'The more you complain, the longer you remain.' I always thought that was a dumb saying until I had to wait for something important, and I complained about it in the waiting process, and it really seemed to make the process much longer.

I guess that's why it tells us in Philippians 2:14, 15 "Do everything without grumbling or arguing, so that you may become blameless and pure, "children of God without fault in a warped and crooked generation. Then you will shine among them like stars in the sky."

I would have never thought that my lack of complaining during the waiting process would be something that would be compared with a light shining through the darkness in the midst of a perverse generation, although I know that a perverse generation exists. I guess our life is a reflection of who we serve, and when we do all waiting without complaining and grumbling, we become like blameless and harmless children who stand out from the norm of those who are always waiting and complaining about their situations.

Isn't it amazing when we look at it that way? Sometimes we think waiting is just waiting, but it's a sign to others of who we are. It's true our actions speak louder than our words.

Got Questions.org tells us, 'The Greek word translated "complainer" means literally "One who is discontented with his lot in life." It's very similar to the word grumbler. Complaining is certainly not a fruit of the Spirit as found in Galatians 5:22, 23 and, in fact, is detrimental to the peace, joy, and patience that come from the Spirit. For the Christian, complaining is damaging and draining, and personally only serves to make our witness to the world more difficult. Who, for instance, would be attracted to a religion whose followers are dissatisfied with life and who continually grumble and complain?

Did you know when we complain or murmur we are actually offending God? After-all, doesn't it say in 2 Corinthians 12:10 "That is why, for Christ's sake, I delight in weaknesses, in insults, in hardships, in persecutions, in difficulties. For when I am weak, then I am strong."

And again in Philippians 4:11 "I am not saying this because I am in need, for I have learned to be content whatever the circumstances." It's also mentioned in Numbers 11:1 "Now the people complained about their hardships in the hearing of the LORD, and when he heard them his anger was aroused. Then fire from the LORD burned among them and consumed some of the outskirts of the camp."

It would seem that when we have to wait longer than we would like we end up complaining about the situation or what we are waiting for, or just having to wait in general.

We live within a society that has become impatient with waiting. We have instant coffee, instant telegrams, instant emails but there is no instant solution for the things that typically cause us to wait. Besides, waiting can be a great time to spend with the Lord, after-all, you don't have anything to do but wait anyway.

Here are a few verses to reflect on while we are in the waiting process,

"The LORD is good to those whose hope is in him, to the one who seeks him," Lamentations 3:25

"For the revelation awaits an appointed time, it speaks of the end and will not prove false. Though it linger, wait for it, it will certainly come and will not delay." Habakkuk 2:3

"Since ancient times no one has heard, no ear has perceived, no eye has seen any God besides you, who acts on behalf of those who wait for him." Isaiah 64:4

Hosea 12:6 "But you must return to your God, maintain love and justice, and wait for your God always.

And the last one, "I wait for your salvation, O Lord." Genesis 49:18

Waiting seems to be something that is inevitable, we will always find ourselves waiting for something or someone. It's how we respond in the waiting process that will either be pleasing or not pleasing to the Lord, the choice is really ours. As I'm fond of saying, 'It's not what you go through that matters but your actions and conduct in the midst of what you go through that makes the difference.'

As stated in Psalms 37:23 "The steps of the righteous are ordered by the Lord." If that be the case then waiting should be seen as something from the Lord and we should thank Him for the opportunity to spend time with Him. Who knows, maybe our waiting time is of the Lord and He is saving us from something that we never saw coming down the road.

Prayer, Father, I don't like waiting, and I really don't like waiting for something that is important, and I have no idea what the outcome will be. Help me to realize that You are in control, and when I acknowledge You in all my ways, you direct my footsteps. Help my waiting to be something that reflects that my trust is in You and You alone.

I Don't Understand

As I was reading in scripture this morning, I came across this verse, which jumped off the page at me, Mark 4:34 "He did not say anything to them without using a parable. But when he was alone with his own disciples, he explained everything."

I can remember very clearly when I was in college taking Organic Chemistry, I would sit in front of the professor as he explained what the lesson of the day was, and I can also remember looking at his mouth as the words came forth, and although I had a pretty good grasp and understanding of the English language, the words that came forth made absolutely no sense to me. He may as well have been speaking in a foreign language; it would have made as much sense to me.

I imagine this would have been the case with the disciples as Jesus was speaking to them about the Kingdom, not only that, He was speaking in parables or as some versions put it in dark sayings. Jesus is speaking of one thing, and He actually is trying to make a reference to something else. I guess this is why it says in Mark 4:33 "With many similar parables Jesus spoke the word to them, as much as they could understand", or in John 10:6 "Jesus used this figure of speech, but the Pharisees did not understand what he was telling them."

I'm pretty sure many must have asked the question, 'What is He talking about, or I have no idea what He's referring to.' The funny thing is that Jesus knew exactly what He was doing, and that this speaking to them in parables was intentional, and one day He would speak in such a way that the meaning would be crystal clear. How do I know this? Because Jesus said so in John 16:25 "Though I have been speaking figuratively, a time is coming when I will no longer use this kind of language but will tell you plainly about my Father."

What exactly is a parable? Wikipedia says 'A parable is a short tale that illustrates a universal truth; it is a simple narrative. It sketches a setting, describes an action, and shows the results. A parable often involves a character who faces a moral dilemma or one who makes a bad decision, and then suffers the unintended consequences. Although the meaning of a parable is often not explicitly stated, it is not intended to be hidden or secret but, on the contrary, quite straightforward and obvious.'

So the next question is, why did Jesus speak in parables? It could be so His enemies wouldn't have anything to arrest Him for. The enemies of Jesus were always waiting for him to say something they could use against him. By speaking in parables, Jesus was making it really hard for them. He couldn't be arrested for telling ordinary stories! Another reason may have been the fact that people like to hear stories rather than a teaching, and Jesus was always speaking to crowds. Another reason would have been the fact that in the crowds, there are all types of people, and some hear a story, another would hear a moral teaching, and another would have the scales fall away from their eyes as Jesus made an earth-shattering statement for some.

How many times have you heard a teaching and suddenly something was said that made you want to rush home and open the word, or you found yourself taking page after page of notes as God made a revelation or illumination of His word or the meaning of a verse.

How many times did you say to yourself, 'I wish I had an opportunity to speak to that professor or that teacher or that preacher, so I could ask him about what he just said?' With that in mind, we come to the basis for this teaching, which is found in Mark 4:34 "He did not say anything to them without using a parable. But when he was alone with his own disciples, he explained everything."

If while you're reading the word or maybe in a busy setting and the Lord begins to reveal something to you, but you have no idea what He's trying to tell you, maybe the key is found in Mark 4:34 but more specifically verse 34b, "But when he was alone with his disciples, he explained everything to them." I believe the key is getting alone with Jesus, so He can explain everything to you.

Jesus was accustomed to getting alone with the Father, as we read in Mark 1:35 "Very early in the morning, while it was still dark, Jesus got up, left the house and went off to a solitary place, where he prayed." Again in Luke 6:12 "One of those days Jesus went out to a mountainside to pray, and spent the night praying to God."

I'm not sure how it happens or the mechanics of how it happens, and truth be told; I really don't care to know the details, but I know beyond a shadow of a doubt that when I get alone with the Lord, many mysteries, or unknowns, or decisions that have to be made, become known to me.

It's like a healing, do you really care how you were healed or are you just so thankful that you or someone you know was healed by the Lord. The details are not as important as the results, and often times the results, and the steps to those results are made known when you're in your secret place or quiet place with the Lord. A quiet place makes room for an intimate place, and you don't have to raise your voice; you don't have to be loud to get someone else's attention, and it's exactly the same spending time with the Lord. When you are alone with the Lord, there's very little competition for the lime-light, you are there to receive, and to be filled with the new things that the Lord has for you.

It's easier to hear someone in a quiet room than in a mall filled with people. Can you imagine trying to carry on an intimate conversation with someone at Times Square on New Year's Eve on Broadway? You would have to scream right in their ear and even then you may not be heard.

But God says 'Get alone with Me and I will tell you all things, especially the things that you don't understand or the things that are confusing you or scare you.' In Jeremiah 29:11 we read, "For I know the plans I have for you," declares the LORD, "plans to prosper you and not to harm you, plans to give you hope and a future." God has great things in store for each one of us, and He wants to let us know what they are so we can be a people of joy. In Psalm 40:5 it states, "Many, LORD my God, are the wonders you have done, the things you planned for us. None can compare with you, were I to speak and tell of your deeds, they would be too many to declare."

When God begins to reveal many of His wonders to us, He doesn't want us cupping our ears because of the background noise, and He certainly doesn't want our busy schedules, programs, and plans to compete with what He wants to say to us. Can God get our attention? Of course He can or it wouldn't tell us in Nahum 1:5 "The mountains

91

quake before him and the hills melt away. The earth trembles at his presence, the world and all who live in it." That sounds like someone who can get our attention. But God would rather the quiet intimate setting of just you and Him where you listen to what it is that He wants to say to you.

Prayer, Lord, I know that you are a speaking God, and You have much to say to me. Help me to take the time to sit at Your feet and open my ears as-well-as my heart to all the mysteries that You want to share with me, and let me not be captivated with the things around me.

I Lift My Eyes to the Hills

I don't know about you, but I am so blessed with Psalm 25:15 "I continually look to the LORD for help, for only he will release my feet from the traps of my enemies."

Have you ever found yourself in a situation where there didn't seem to be any way out? I mean a situation that no matter how hard you looked for a solution to the issue; you couldn't humanely figure out how to bring closure to what seemed like a really dark cloud that was just hanging over your head.

I remember once going through a really difficult time in a situation that was not of my choosing, and I thought I knew the solutions to get out of the condition, but the more I tried to make it happen in my own strength, the deeper I seemed to sink into the quicksand of the issue. It was so bad; I found myself repenting for things I didn't even do hoping that maybe there were secret sins in my life that I would catch in my 'Repent for everything' episode, and the issue would be solved.

I was quoting scripture, reminding God of His promises, and claiming everything the bible had to offer in order to come through this dark tunnel in my life.

Strange, looking back over the entire incident today, it seems the problem was really not that bad, and I had made a mountain out of a mole hill as the expression goes. Have any of you experienced the mountain out of a mole hill issue, or a small breeze of discomfort that you turned into a major category 5 hurricane in your life?

You see my friends; it's not only the actual issue that causes the fear or confusion, but where you put your eyes and what you do or don't do that will either magnify or diminish the winds and waves of the storms of life. Peter is an example of that in Matthew 14:30-32 "But seeing the wind, he became frightened, and beginning to sink, he cried out, "Lord, save me!" Immediately Jesus stretched out His hand and took hold of him, and said to him, "You of little faith, why did you doubt?" When they got into the boat, the wind stopped."

'Lord save me' may be the shortest prayer in the bible with wonderful results. Peter was sinking into the water, and the last thing on his mind was a five-page discourse on the molecular structure of water. Lord save me really sums it all up. It's a great example of James 4:2b "You do not have, because you do not ask God."

Why is this prayer such an excellent example of how to pray? For one, it takes your eyes off of the original problem, the winds of life and puts them on the only One who can deliver you, Jesus. It puts everything in perspective; I am in need of being saved, and you are a savior, what a perfect match made in heaven.

Let's face it; problems exist and none of us can escape them. In Psalm 73:14 it says, "All day long I have been afflicted, and every morning brings new punishments." To make matters worse, look at this in Ecclesiastes 8:14 "There is something else meaningless that occurs on earth, the righteous who get what the wicked deserve, and the wicked who get what the righteous deserve."

The issue my friends are not will I have problems; you can be assured you will have them; the issue is, where do you put your eyes when they come, which brings me to the heart of this message, Psalm 25:15 "I continually look to the LORD for help, for only he will release my feet from the traps of my enemies?" Another way of expressing this is Psalm 121:1 "I lift up my eyes to the hills. From where does my help come," or Psalm 120:1 "In my distress, I cried to the LORD, and he heard me."

Many of the problems of life take us by surprise because in most cases, we are not expecting them, but they don't take the Lord by surprise, because God and only God knows the ending from the beginning, besides, "A person's steps are directed by the LORD, and the LORD delights in his way according to Psalm 37:23."

I think we all know that we cannot live in a protective shell or a bubble that will protect us from the issues of life, but we can continually look to the Lord for help. We can lift our eyes to the hills where our help comes from, and we can cry to the Lord knowing that our cries don't fall on deaf ears but on a loving, faithful God that hears every cry of His children, and even before we cry out for help God already knew the desire of our hearts, and is already sending help our way. If it were not so why would Psalm 34:17 encourage us with "The righteous cry out, and the LORD hears them, he delivers them from all their troubles."

Did you know that in many cases, God desires to answer our cry and deliver us more than we want to cry out for help? For this reason, I would like to echo the truthful statement in Deuteronomy 4:7 "What other nation is so great as to have their gods near them the way the LORD our God is near us whenever we pray to him?"

My friends, don't be slow in calling out to a Heavenly Father who already knows what you need before you know what the problem is.

Prayer: Gracious, loving Father, many times the winds and waves of life are so over whelming, and when I look directly at them, they seem to be without a solution. Help me to lift my eyes to the hills where my help comes from, and that is to put my eyes on the Lord my God, who has and is the solution to all the problems.

It Is What It Is

Today's inspiration is dedicated to a dear friend of ours who lives in the Blue Ridge Mountains of Georgia. The title 'It is what it is' I'm happy to say, is the expression our dear friend uses often, and we were even able to purchase a sign that said, 'It Is What It Is.'

So what exactly does the expression it is what it is mean, and what if any spiritual application can be learned from it?

It would seem the meaning of this expression is that things are exactly as they seem to be. Personally, it can be a statement of faith or an act of giving up, and it doesn't take into account anything other than the face value of where you are at the moment.

Example, a person might say, 'Although the doctors tell me there is no hope for my getting well, the word of God tells me that I have been healed, and I believe the word of God, so it is what it is and I will stand on the word of God.' Someone else might say 'Everything in my family is falling apart and no matter what I do the situation doesn't get any better, and it is what it is, so I will just let the pieces fall where they fall, and try to put all the pieces together another time.' It would seem to me that, it is what it is depends on who you are, and what firm foundation you are standing upon at the time. One thing is very clear; it is what it is does not take into account the power to call the things which are as if they were not.

With God, it is what it is takes on an entirely different meaning. For example, in Genesis 1:1 we are told, "In the beginning God created the heavens and the earth." There's no introduction to God, no explanation of where God came from, and no debate if God exists or not. Why? Because God doesn't need an introduction or an explanation. You see; with God, it is what it is.

Again in John 1:1 - 4 we are told, "In the beginning was the Word, and the Word was with God, and the Word was fully God. The Word was with God in the beginning. All things were created by him, and apart from him not one thing was created that has been created. In him was life, and the life was the light of mankind." My friends, we see that in the beginning or eternal past, there was God, and He was the Word, and that Word had a name, and that name is Jesus, the name above all names, and that name created everything that was, is, or ever hopes to be because it is what it is, and that name is the life and light of all mankind.

Again, no introduction or explanation, because it is what it is and that's the end to the debate and closure.

That's God, but we already knew that. But what about us, the children of God? Sometimes we feel saved sometimes we don't, sometimes we feel holy, other times we don't, sometimes we feel like more than conquerors, other times we don't. Sometimes we feel like we can do all things through Christ Jesus, and other times we don't, sometimes we really do feel like the head and other times we feel like the tail.

So the issue of it is what it is, does that apply to us, the children of the living God, does it truthfully apply to our situations? No! Absolutely not because we don't live our lives based on feelings but on the promises and the Word of God knowing that God is faithful to a thousand generations.

You see my friends; we are not what we think we are, but we are what we think. We are who God says we are, and that my friend is what it is.

So next time you find yourself in a situation that seems really hopeless and there doesn't seem to be a way out of your lion's den experience or fiery furnace, don't ever settle for your current situation but continue to push on to the greater revelations of God in your life. You do not have to settle for it is what it is because of one main reason, and that my friend is He is who He said He is, our Heavenly Father and He is still the Great I Am.

Prayer, Lord, sometimes I see the wind and wave situations in my life, and I fall into the trap of believing that it is the way it is, and there's no way out. Help me to see beyond the circumstances and situations of my life and bring me to a place where I can believe that what You say is the way it is, and that there is always hope for a better outcome to my life.

It's Not For You

It's truly a blessing to be able to participate in so many different services and hear praise and worship in so many different languages.

So the question becomes, what exactly is praise and worship? According to Steve Ham in 'What is praise?' Steve tells us, 'Praise is a response of worship. We sing boasts about the greatness of our God with purity and vigor. We proclaim His greatness to others in joy and excitement. We spread words of comfort to the afflicted as we declare His goodness and sovereignty. We can confidently boast about our God in all situations.'

So if that's praise, what is worship? Delesslyn A. Kennebrew in 'What is True Worship' tells us, 'True worship, is defined by the priority we place on who God is in our lives and where God is on our list of priorities. True worship is a matter of the heart expressed through a lifestyle of holiness.'

So we see there is a significant difference in the meaning of praise and worship, but what does the word of God have to say about praise and worship? In Psalm 150 it encourages us with, "Praise the Lord. Praise God in His sanctuary, praise Him in His mighty heavens. Praise Him for his acts of power, praise Him for his surpassing greatness. Praise Him with the sounding of the trumpet, praise Him with the harp and lyre, praise Him with the timbrel, which is a small hand drum or tambourine, and dancing, praise Him with the strings and pipe, praise Him with the clash of cymbals, praise Him with resounding cymbals. Let everything that has breath praise the Lord. Praise the Lord." In John 4:23 we read, "But the time is coming, indeed it's here now, when true worshipers will worship the Father in spirit and in truth. The Father is looking for those who will worship him that way."

Now that we have a little clearer understanding of what praise and worship is, we go back to our travels around the world. We have had the joy of praising and worshipping God in various countries and in diverse languages. In Israel, we praise and worship in English, Hebrew and Arabic. In Germany, we praise and worship God in German. We have heard praise and worship in Spanish, French, Italian, Korean and many other languages. We have praised and worshipped God in contemporary style, hymns, country, rap and the list goes on and on.

In addition, we are told in Psalm 149:3 "Let them praise his name in the dance, let them sing praises to him with the tambourine and harp."

Psalm 150:4 "Praise him with the tambourine and dance, praise him with stringed instruments and organs."

Here's where I bring all this together and make my point. It never fails, that wherever we go, we hear someone say, I didn't like the praise, or I didn't like the worship; it was too fast, or it was too slow, or it was too modern, or I don't like all those instruments, or I didn't like the way that person was dancing in the isle or waving that flag around and how about this one, it didn't do anything for me. As I read all these scriptures, I've come to realize something; praise and worship isn't for us, it's for Him.

Is it an option to praise and worship God? No, it's a command. We are told that God is the focus of our devotion in both the Old Testament and the New Testament. In Exodus 20:2-3 God says, "I am the LORD your God...You shall have no other gods before me." In Matthew 4:10 Jesus says, "Worship the Lord your God and serve him only." So worship is not merely a natural instinct, it's a command from God. Not only that, but we're instructed in Psalm 22:3 "But you are holy, you who inhabit the praises of Israel." You know, another meaning for inhabit is populate, reside or dwell. So if one day you feel that God is far away just begin to praise Him because it would seem that praise gets His attention, and He likes to reside where the praise is. Why do you think God would do that? That's simple, because He loves our praise and worship.

Now for a scary thought. God says He loves our praise and worship in every form, from singing to dance to clapping and waving banners; He loves it so much that God actually decides that He wants to dwell right in the midst of it, and we say I don't like the praise and worship. I don't know about you, but I don't think it's a good idea to tell God that I don't like what you like, and we are told in Amos 3:3 "Can two walk together, except they are in agreement?" In other words, if you like what God likes or you don't like what God doesn't like, that is called agreement, but if you like what God doesn't like or don't like what God likes, there is a problem. As I am so very fond of saying, 'If my hand hits the wall or the wall hits my hand, regardless, my hand will lose.'

You see, if what you're looking for is Hollywood entertainment, going to church isn't the solution, that's why they have movies or the theatre, so you can be entertained. However, if you are looking for the presence of God, granted you might find it in the movies like the wonderful 2014 movie we just saw called God's Not Dead, by Harold Cronk and released by Pure Flix Entertainment or the movie called Heaven Is for Real, based on a 2010 book by Todd Burpo and Lynn Vincent and released by Sony Pictures.

The presence of God is not a matter of location but a matter of the heart. If you are in a service and the music isn't to your liking, or you see someone dancing before the Lord like David danced before the Lord, and you don't like it, the problem might be, the music or dancing is not for you, it's for God, or your eyes are on the wrong person, and you came to receive or be entertained rather than give unto the Lord.

By the way, the last issue is an easy fix. If you put your eyes on Him and He shows up because He loves praise and worship, you now find yourself in the presence of God and a person cannot leave the same way after being in His presence. Before I forget, saying that you don't like the praise and worship or saying it does nothing for me after looking at the way others praise and worship is just another way of despising the worship from a distance, and we know what happens when you do that. Let's read in 2 Samuel 6:14,16,23 "Wearing a linen ephod, David was dancing before the Lord with all his might, while he and all Israel were bringing up the ark of the Lord with shouts and the sound of trumpets. As the ark of the Lord was entering the City of David, Michal daughter of Saul watched from a window. And when she saw King David leaping and dancing before the Lord, she despised him from afar in her heart. And Michal daughter of Saul was barren to the day of her death." You see my friends, despising from afar what God holds dear to His heart can have really bad consequences.

Since I don't want to leave you on a negative note, let me explain exactly what praise and worship do, praise elevates us into God's presence and power, praise sends the enemy running, and praise is an expression of faith and a declaration of victory! It declares that we believe God is with us and is in control of the outcome of all our circumstances.

Prayer, Father, help me to realize that not all things are about me or have to be about me and what I want but about You and always have been about You and always will be about You.

Let Go and Let God

I've heard the expression 'Let Go and Let God' for such a long time, especially when dealing with tough or trying situations.

You know, sometimes we hear something so often that we begin to believe that it's from the bible. Example, cleanliness is next to Godliness. It sounds really scriptural but the truth is it's not to be found throughout the bible at all. According to English Language and Usage, It was first found among the writings of Phinehas ben Yair, an ancient rabbi.

So what exactly does Let Go and Let God mean? Dorothy M. Neddermeyer PhD, in her article 'Let Go and Let God' describes it this way, 'Let go and let God is a phrase people frequently use. At times, it seems more of a cliché than an intention of action. Ponder that phrase for a moment. What does let go and let God mean? Does it mean that God will appear in your house or at work to do all the things in your life that need to be done? Or does it mean that you need to allow yourself to connect with the God within so that the God within can assist you in accomplishing what you want to accomplish.'

Personally, I've heard both extremes where people will either completely do nothing, or expect God to do it all, or the people will do everything, and if it goes wrong, let God clean up their mess. Unfortunately, both extremes are completely wrong.

Can you imagine if Peter in Matthew 14:28 where he walked on the water choose either of these two extremes? One extreme would be Lord if it's really you, why don't you walk over to the boat, reach inside, pick me up and carry me on the water and gently put me down until I can stand on the water by myself? The other extreme would be Lord, hold on I'm coming, and with reckless abandonment jump out of the boat regardless of the situation and circumstances around him.

You see; first Peter confirmed that it was the Lord. Next he asked permission to join the Lord where He was, namely on the water. Thirdly, Peter didn't do anything until he had the invitation to "come" and lastly Peter himself had to make the effort to get out of the boat and stand on the water keeping his eyes on the Lord at all times. The moment he took his eyes off the Lord he began to sink. The water hadn't changed; Peter hadn't changed; the Lord didn't change, and so what caused Peter from walking on the water to sinking in the water? It's where he put his eyes.

How many times do we take our eyes off the Lord, who is our source of our faith and placed them on the situation which is our source of little faith? The result obviously being doubt. We doubt ourselves; we doubt the Lord; we doubt our victory, and we doubt the faithful promises of God.

Whenever the problems are bigger than the promises, we have a serious issue.

I've heard people say, and I'm guilty of the saying myself, when our vertical relationship is healthy, our horizontal relationships will be healthy. That sounds great but it still

106

reflects one of the extremes, namely, let go and let God. In other words, we can have a wonderful relationship with God, but if we don't personally do something to try and better the horizontal relationships around us, we still have a serious problem.

Example, we can have a wonderful relationship with God, but if we don't clean our house, it will be an absolute mess.

On the other hand, we can have an amazingly clean house, the talk of everyone that sees it, and yet be spiritually empty or what Paul describes as giving the impression of Godliness. In other words, and we've all heard this expression, 'We become so heavenly minded that we become no earthly good.'

So what's the solution? I would venture to say that it's a two-fold solution. We need to press into the deeper things of God, that's an obvious place to start, but next I think we need to be sensitive to the people around us; their wants, needs, and likes, and try to do what it takes to fill those voids in their lives.

Example, in a marriage, if a person doesn't like oatmeal for breakfast, although it's very healthy, and you just happen to love oatmeal, don't always make oatmeal for breakfast. Find out what the other person likes and make that. There are so many examples of what a little sensitivity will do and how far it can take you in learning how to bend over backwards for the other person. I'm sure it will have a wonderful return on its investment. This is what I like to call life balance.

In addition, there is what I like to call spiritual balance. In our spiritual walk, a good example of spiritual balance can be found in 2 Corinthians 10:5 which says, "Casting down imaginations, that's reasoning, and every high thing that exalts itself against the knowledge of God, and bringing into captivity every thought, that's perception, purpose and intellect to the obedience, and that means compliance and submission of and to Christ."

So if we put the whole thing together what does the picture look like? How do we combine life balance and spiritual balance? Well, it looks like a person who is pressing into the deeper things of God. For some, this might mean regular early-morning prayer time with The Lord, or evening bible studies for others, or an all-day Christ-centered, God-fearing awareness for some. How or when we press into the Lord is not as important as determining that we will press into the Lord. And balancing this with being sensitive to others around us, their likes, needs, wants, and dislikes. In other words, it's very possible to be Godly and human at the same time. I realize that sounds strange, but I also realize you know exactly what I'm speaking about. We have all come across someone in our life that seems to be from another world or out of touch with reality. The problem is they have not learned how to combine the life balance with the spiritual balance resulting in being off balance or out of balance.

The answer can be summed up in 2 Corinthians 8:14 where Paul is speaking to the brethren at the congregation of Macedonia. Some have an abundance of what is needed and others are lacking what is needed, so Paul makes this statement, "But by an equality, that now at this time your lavishness may be a supply for their absence that their abundance also may be a supply for your neediness, the result being that there may be fairness or a balance."

As we press into the deeper things of God vertically, we also need to press into being part of the solution, not the problem horizontally. Find out what others like or don't like and be an instrument to fill that need.

Prayer, Gracious Father, Help me to be sensitive to those around me and not to be caught up in the hustle and bustle of life and realize that I am Your hands and feet where You have planted me. Help me to be a sweet fragrance to those I come in contact with.

Let the Main Thing be the Main Thing

Not too long ago I had the opportunity to watch a 1991 re-run movie called City Slickers directed by Ron Underwood and released by Columbia Pictures. The stars of the movie were Billy Crystal, named Mitch, a New Yorker going through a midlife crisis and Jack Palance, named Curly, a tough-as-nails trails boss. In one scene, we discover that Curly is more than just a trail boss cowboy with a tough exterior, but that he is a very wise man. In this scene Curly advises Mitch how to face his problems, by singling out the "main thing" that is most important in life, and says to Mitch "let the main thing be the main thing" to which Mitch asks, "what is the main thing?" to which Curly says, "Ah, that's what you have to find out."

That scene has always stuck with me because therein lies the joy of life. So what is the main thing? Sometimes life has us prioritizing life in more than just A, B, C but in 1A, 2A, 3A because there are issues in our lives that are really super important, and it would seem that they are all at the top of the list. I mean how you prioritize your family, your job, your spouse, your health, your walk with God and the list goes on and on? Really, if it were as easy as my walk with God or painting my kitchen, that would be worry-free, but life is not that easy, and sometimes situations, people and life all compete for my number-one position at the 1A level.

I once did a paper that was titled, 'What do you do when you get to the top of the ladder of success only to find it's leaning on the wrong wall.' We have all seen this story unfold on the incredibly successful businessman or doctor or the lawyer who looks back over his life of success and finds his marriage on the rocks, his children involved in drugs, his friends all gone and although successful, he is totally alone in life.

The question becomes what was his main thing and the question for you my friend is what is your main thing in life? No one starts out in life with a plan to destroy their marriage by being too busy to care, or no one starts a family saying 'I think I'll let my children go to ruin in about 15 years.' We all start with great and good intentions, but somewhere in life something happens and the main thing was forced out, and became a minor thing in life.

Look at Matthew 14:28-30 "Peter said to Him, "Lord, if it is You, command me to come to You on the water." And He said, "Come!" And Peter got out of the boat, and walked on the water and came toward Jesus. But seeing the wind, he became frightened, and beginning to sink, he cried out, "Lord, save me!" You would think the main thing for Peter was to save his own life from drowning, and if we were in his shoes that would probably be our main thing, but the main thing was to keep your eyes on Jesus who according to Hebrews 12:2 "Is the author and finisher of our faith."

You see; Jesus didn't rebuke Peter because he couldn't swim or stay afloat, Jesus rebuked Peter for his little faith. If Jesus is the author and finisher of our faith that means that God started it, and He will maintain it, and He will finish it.

111

The problem as I see it, is that we all have faith the size of a mustard seed to move the mountain, but we try to drum up faith the size of the mountain to move the mustard seed. We got it all wrong.

So what is the main thing? According to Romans 8:1 "Now the main thing of what we are saying is this, We have such a high priest, one who sat down at the right hand of the throne of the Majesty in heaven." In other words, the main thing is not a place nor is it a thing nor is it anything that is man-made. For believers, the main thing in life has to be a person, and that person has a name, and that name is above all other names in heaven, and on earth and that name is Jesus.

When you keep your eyes on Jesus, the main thing for your life or your ladder to success will be on the right wall, and your family will be a God-fearing, Christ-centered joy to be around, your home will be a place of rest, and a sanctuary of God's presence, a place where you look forward to being in and not escaping from.

With Jesus as the main thing of your life, you don't have to worry about Him being your bridge over troubled waters; He dries up the troubled waters, and you pass over on dry ground. Is that true you might be asking yourself? In Exodus 14:22 it tells us "And the people of Israel went into the midst of the sea on dry ground, the waters being a wall to them on their right hand and on their left." Again in Joshua 3:17 "The priests who carried the ark of the covenant of the LORD stopped in the middle of the Jordan and stood on dry ground, while all Israel passed by until the whole nation had completed the crossing on dry ground."

Since God is not a respecter of persons, and the same yesterday, today and forever, that means what He has done for one he will do for others.

So back to City Slickers where Curly advises Mitch how to face his problems, by singling out the "main thing" that is most important in life and says to Mitch "let the main thing be the main thing" to which Mitch asks, "what is the main thing?" and Curly says, "Ah, that's what you have to find out." Here's the good news my friends, I found out what is the main thing, and it's Jesus, King of Kings and Lord of Lords.

Prayer, Lord, I have so many things that are so important to me and my family and life, but help me to realize that there is only one main thing in life that I have to focus on, and that's You Lord.

Life Is a Puzzle

The other day Norma and I were saying good-bye to a friend, and this friend mentioned something to Norma that really stood out in my mind. She said 'Now that we have met you, you have become pieces in my puzzle of life.' I found this to be very interesting and Norma received further revelation to this statement when she mentioned to me that life was like a puzzle, and all the pieces are present, it's just that they have not yet been put together to form the bigger picture. What wonderful insight.

Dictionary.com tells us that 'A puzzle is something designed to amuse by presenting difficulties to be solved by patient effort.' What is a puzzle exactly if not a mystery? We all know that a mystery is anything that is kept secret or remains unexplained or unknown. Many mysteries could never be revealed unless it came from the Revealer of all mysteries.

What this friend told Norma was 'All the mysteries of life or puzzle pieces are present it's just that we have not placed them on the board of life.'

When I was a teenager, my older brother use to love putting these one thousand piece puzzles together. I never had the patience for that, but I did have a knack for really up-setting my brother by always taking three or four pieces and hiding them. After threating my life a few times for pulling this prank on him, I promised never to remove puzzle pieces again. What I discovered was, having too many pieces is just as annoying as too few pieces, soooo, I use to find pieces that looked like they belonged in the puzzle and added five or six pieces that didn't belong to his puzzle. This used to drive my brother right up the wall.

Life is like a puzzle. Many of the pieces are out there, it's just that we haven't come across them yet. Although they belong in our puzzle of life, they have yet to be discovered. Not only that, many of the pieces are irregular and have to be turned this way and that way before they fit. Other pieces look like they fit, but they belong in a different place on the playing field of life. And then there are the pieces that we have no idea what to do with them, and that requires divine intervention as Daniel 2:19 tells us, "During the night the mystery was revealed to Daniel in a vision." In other words, this part of the puzzle of life needs help and as Daniel 2:27, 28 says, "No wise man, enchanter, magician or diviner can explain to the King the mystery he has asked about, but, thank God for the word but, in Hebrew it's the word Bram and means 'Only or nevertheless', there is a God in heaven who reveals mysteries."

Just to be certain, when I speak about the puzzles of life, I'm speaking about people, places, and things.

Something else I use to do to my brother which was really, really nasty. I use to find a puzzle piece that didn't belong in the puzzle, and I molded it to fit in a certain place in the board so that when he placed the piece exactly where it was to go, it was completely out of place. Example, I would cut out a black puzzle piece that fit in a bright blue sky. Right place, wrong color, confusing image, not to mention my brother would threaten my life when he found out what I was doing.

You know, there are times in life when we come across people, places or things that our first impression is to chuck it out because it doesn't fit into our well-organized playing field called life. If that happens, you are doing to yourself what I use to do to my brother, and that is to hide pieces, which really meant the complete picture of life will be incomplete. In addition, if a person, place or thing doesn't belong in your puzzle of life, don't try to force it in place by cutting corners, you might make it fit, but it will be awkward, out of place, and confusing in your life's picture.

The perfect life picture for each of us is the picture that the Lord has pre-planned for us. Jeremiah 29:11 It tells us, "For I know the plans I have for you, declares the Lord, plans to prosper you and not to harm you, plans to give you hope and a future." In other words, the Lord is telling us that He has the perfect life's picture for us. Every person, place or thing that He has placed on our path is vital to the bigger picture, and not only vital but necessary. One thing I know for certain, every piece that the Lord places in our path of life is not going to make us immediately joyful.

Personally, how many times had a person, place or thing also known as a puzzle piece of my life been a major thorn in my side only to discover that somewhere down the road I realized how important it really was? I guess that's what I call jumping at a conclusion. However, God tells us in Isaiah 55:8, indeed, "My plans are not like your plans, and My deeds are not like your deeds." You know, if our plans and deeds were like the Lord's plans and deeds, our life's puzzle would be perfect in every aspect.

Let's be real, for all of us; we all have a puzzle called life, and for some, it may be almost completely filled in and for others maybe half way and some have a few pieces in place with many more pieces to meet, but it's our life, and we are trying to do the best we can with what we got. With that, I will paraphrase Proverbs 19:21, "There are many plans to fill our puzzle of life with what we have in mind, and with the pieces that we think or feel might fit, but it is the counsel of the Lord, who will determine, which is the right piece for our life."

Prayer, Father, sometimes life seems to be like juggling many things in the air at the same time, and more often than not, something gets dropped or misplaced. Help me Lord to allow You to determine what are the pieces that I need to live my life and still be pleasing to You.

No Power on Earth

Today's sharing is a little different if I must say so myself. I'm sitting in the back yard of a dear couple here in Virginia. It's raining and a little on the cool side, and I thought I would share on one thing, and it would seem the Lord would have me share on something that wasn't even in my mind. I really can't wait to see how this turns out.

You know how we are told in 2 Timothy 3:16 "That all Scripture is inspired by God and is useful to teach us what is true and to make us realize what is wrong in our lives. It corrects us when we are wrong and teaches us to do what is right."

Interesting, the Word of God is inspired or another word for inspired is stirred, or motivated by the Breath of God, or as we say in Hebrew, the Ruaach HaKodesh, the Holy Spirit. We are told in Psalm 51:11 "Do not cast me from your presence or take your Holy Spirit from me." Why would the writer of this Psalm say what he just said? Because Job 33:4 tells us, "The Spirit of God has made me, and the breath of the Almighty gives me life."

Have you ever thought that you really knew something but the realization of what you thought you knew begins to dawn upon you? Do you realize that the breath of God, and the Spirit of God, and the Spirit of the Lord God, are all capable of doing different things in the life of a believer? If not why would Job say, "The Spirit of God has made me, and the Breath of the Almighty gives me life?"

As I'm sitting here in the backyard putting together my thoughts, and still recuperating from my surgery, at one point, I had a very healthy yawn from being a little tired due to not sleeping well at night. Did I pay much attention to it? Not really, until I realized it was the breath of Don. Was there anything special about that breath of Don, of course not?

What I realized is the breath of Don is evidence of life, but the Breath of God gives life. And by the way, the Breath of God is not a onetime transaction but a continuous operation of a life-giving process. One other very important issue to think about, in ancient Hebrew, there's a saying, 'He who breathes of himself breathes of his essence.' In Genesis 2:7 it tells us "Then the LORD God formed the man from the dust of the ground. He breathed the breath of life into the man's nostrils, and the man became a living person."

Listen to this, a potter will fashion clay into the shape he desires; the Lord took the dust and clay of the Earth, and formed man into what He desired. Then He breathed life into his nostrils. This breath became the spirit of man, complete with its own will, its intellect, reason, and its ability for morals and fellowship with the Creator who formed him.

So an important question becomes, what is the essence of God? By the way, essence means the core, or soul, or heart, in other words, what is the core, or soul, or heart of God? Once we understand that, we will understand that the DNA of God is now pulsating in the DNA of man, the core or soul or heart of God now becomes the core or soul or heart of man. Why is this significant? Because the human body, as intricate and magnificently made as it is, is not what defines a person, it's this spirit which God breathed into man who defines a person. It's this spirit, which bears the image and likeness of God.

It's the reason why when we enter a room, we bring the presence of God, and cause a change in that room. It's the reason that Paul said in Galatians 2:20 "I have been crucified with Christ and I no longer live, but Christ lives in me." It's the same reason why in I Corinthians 3:16 we are told, "Don't you know that you yourselves are God's temple and that God's Spirit dwells in your midst?" Again in Romans 8:11 "And if the Spirit of Him who raised Jesus from the dead is living in you, He who raised Christ from the dead will also give life to your mortal bodies because of his Spirit who lives in you."

So you see my friends, it's not who we are but who He is that makes the difference. If there's one thing that I've learned in 34 years of serving the Lord it's this, I can't save anyone, I can't heal anyone, but He who lives in me can. So when I enter a room, I pray Lord make me invisible so all they can see is You.

For others to see Christ in me is not only what I pray for, but it also takes a heavy weight off of my shoulders because I no longer have to perform or try to make things happen. It's true what we heard when they say 'God's not interested in my great ability but my availability.' As it tells us in Isaiah 6:8 "Then I heard the voice of the Lord saying, "Whom shall I send? And who will go for us?" And I said, "Here am I. Send me!" It doesn't say here I am Lord; I have such great talents and abilities and for sure, I'm the guy, who can get the job done. This is pride, and as James 4:6 reads "Therefore it says, "God opposes the proud, but gives grace to the humble." Grace my friends' means, beauty, loveliness or refinement.

You know, it's never about us but always about Him. As a matter-of-fact, it's consistently been about Him, is about Him and will always be about Him, and that my friends covered the past, the present, and the future, and I don't know of anything that exists outside the past, present and future.

Prayer, Heavenly Father, I ask that You would cause the scales to fall from my eyes that I might see You clearly, and realize that everything I have, You gave me, but You haven't given me everything that You have. Help to make me more available for Your purposes.

One Day

I was sitting listening to Don Potter from the album
Returning and the Lord, blessed be His name, gave me a
word, and it was 'One day'. That's all He said, 'One day.'
Now I have enough experience and insight to realize that
God has a lot more for me than just the word, 'One day.'

 So as I waited upon the Lord, He began to put all the
pieces of the puzzle together in my mind until it was crystal
clear how this meaning was to develop.

We have all experienced that special day in our lives,
which has brought us great joy. You know what I mean,
perhaps it was a vacation trip, and as you counted down the
days until you caught that plane or that cruise ship to your
destination. possibly your one day was the day you got
married, or graduated from high school, or college, or
graduate school. Maybe your one day was when you got
that dream job, and it was your first day on the job. Your
special day could even be the day the doctors said the
cancer was completely gone, or your children came to the
Lord.

We have all experienced that special day moment, and truth
be told, we probably have had many one special day
experiences, and you know something; my special one day
doesn't have to be the same as your special one-day
experience. In other words, what brought me great joy

doesn't necessarily have to be what brings you great joy. I can rejoice with you in that special day that has dawned upon you but not necessarily want what you got.

And you know; concerning our friends, we are not to judge what their one-day experience was. Example, recently I purchased my first radio controlled remote control tank; I was really joyful with that toy. Someone asked me when are you going to grow up? 'Never! No, not ever was my reply.' After all, doesn't Matthew 18:3 tell us "Truly I tell you, unless you change and become like children." Now, I understand that means to grow up and be like a child when it comes to trusting. Did my getting that tank bring them joy? Probably not, and you know something; I didn't care. I didn't get it to make them happy; it was my one-day experience.

I've discovered that not all things that make a person happy or joyful will make everyone happy or joyful. As a matter-of-fact, there will never be a one-day experience that will make everyone happy or joyful.

I said all that to say this, there is a day coming that will be the ultimate one-day experience. There will be a day that according to Revelation 19:11-16 which says, "I saw heaven standing open and there before me was a white horse, whose rider is called Faithful and True. With justice he judges and makes war. His eyes are like blazing fire, and on his head are many crowns. He has a name written on him that no one knows but He himself. He is dressed in a robe dipped in blood, and his name is the Word of God. The armies of heaven were following him, riding on white horses and dressed in fine linen, white and clean. Out of his mouth comes a sharp sword with which to strike down the nations. "He will rule them with an iron scepter." He treads the winepress of the fury of the wrath of God

Almighty. On his robe and on his thigh he has this name written, King of Kings and Lord of Lords." Now that's what I call a day.

Between you and me, that day is going to be a Great Day experience. Is it going to bring me great joy? You bet. Is it going to bring the entire world great joy? I seriously doubt it. Look what it tells us in Revelation 1:7 "Look, He comes with the clouds of heaven. And everyone will see him--even those who pierced him. And all the nations of the world will mourn for him. Yes! Amen!"

How come some of us will be joyful and others unhappy? That's easy, because of verses like I Thessalonians 4:17 "After that, we who are still alive and are left will be caught up together with them in the clouds to meet the Lord in the air. And so we will be with the Lord forever."

Knowing that we belong to Him, and that He has a one-day experience the likes of which we have never experienced, should create within us a joyful anticipation and expectation that He is coming back soon. You might ask yourself, 'What is that day going to look like.' The answer can only come from scripture where it tells us in I Corinthians 2:9 and Isaiah 64:4, "What no eye has seen, what no ear has heard, and what no human mind has conceived." In other words, when it comes to one-day experiences, you haven't seen anything yet.

Your trip to Disney, your dream job came true, your marriage or your graduation is a great and wonderful one-day experience, but 'The day' that the Lord has planned for us is not of this world, and it's not natural, it's supernatural, and what a day that will be. Why? Because many of our one-day experiences often times have some form of disappointment in them. Maybe Disney got rained out, or prices were so high you couldn't do all the things you planned on doing, or your dream job wasn't a dream after all but a nightmare, or your graduation now means you have to start looking for a job, and jobs are hard to find.

What oftentimes seems like a joy, for the moment, turns into weeping due to unfulfilled expectations, or shattered hopes but Psalm 30:5b tells us "Weeping may remain for a night, but rejoicing comes in the morning."

My friends, there is a glorious day coming soon, the likes of which, we who belong to the Lord have never experienced. On that day, there will be no disappointment, no unfulfilled expectations, no weeping, and no regrets.

When will that special day happen, many are asking across the world? Revelation 22:7, 12, 20 All say the same thing, "Look, I am coming soon." Do we know the exact date, of course not, if we did we wouldn't have a hope because we would already know, but we do have a faith that He is coming back soon, and that will be the greatest day in the history of the world. Many will rejoice and many will mourn, but that day is coming never-the-less.

Thank God that we are on the side that will rejoice when He comes, and we will see Him face-to-face. What a day that will be.

Prayer, Father, I have had so many expectations in life that were supposed to be wonderful and joyfully great days, which have turned in to a day of weeping. Help me to realize that You have plans for my life that will bring true joy and peace, and that You have never, and will never fail me.

Peek-A-Boo, I See You

What a strange title for a lesson, and I'm sure most of you are asking yourself what is this message going to be about after seeing a title like that. To answer that question, let me say it comes from two scriptures one in Exodus 2:12 and the other in Psalm 11:4.

In Exodus 2:12 concerning Moses, it tells us "After looking in all directions to make sure no one was watching; Moses killed the Egyptian and hid the body in the sand." You see; the problem was; Moses looked to the left and to the right and probably all around him, but he never looked up.

How many times have we made a decision to do something and looked in all directions to make sure it was the right decision, or the most profitable decision, or the most careful decision, but afterwards we realized it was the wrong decision.

I'm sure based on emotions or feelings we even go so far as to say, Lord, I'm going to do this, and I would like you to bless it. Even so, without doubt, the worst thing we can do is decide because we think the Lord isn't watching or doesn't care what we are doing. In Ezekiel 9:9b we see an example of this very thinking when it says, "They think that the LORD has abandoned the land and that he doesn't see."

126

This brings me to the second scripture that inspired the title of this message, in Psalm 11:4 "The Lord is in his holy temple. The Lord sits on his throne in heaven. He sees everything that happens; He watches people closely."

Let me repeat that because it's extremely important, "He sees everything that happens, and He watches people," that's you and me, and He watches us very closely. God even repeats this often. In Jeremiah 7:11 "Look, I'm watching, declares the LORD," and again in Proverbs 15:3 "The LORD is watching everywhere, keeping his eye on both the evil and the good."

In other words, when we do something or anything, and we feel that God is not interested or watching us, there's a gentle voice that tells us 'Peek-a-boo, I see you. I see everything that you're doing even before you do it, I hear every thought you are thinking. I know everything that you have done, are doing, and will ever do. When I say that 'I will never forsake you or abandon you,' what part of never do you not understand?'

In order to understand the entire concept of peek-a-boo, I see you, we are told in Wikipedia that 'Peek-a-boo is a game played primarily with babies. In the game, the older player hides their face, pops back into the baby's view, and says Peekaboo! Sometimes followed by I see you! It's more than just a fun game; Peek-a-boo is thought by developmental psychologists to demonstrate an infant's inability to understand object permanence.' Wow, that's a big word but what it means is the understanding that objects continue to exist even when they cannot be observed, which is the same as seen, heard, touched, smelled or sensed in any way.

It would seem that Moses and many of us believers concerning God have an issue with object permanence, in other words; we forget that God is always present regardless if you can see Him, feel Him, or sense Him in any way.

I told this personal experience before, but it's so important that I would like to share it again. It was in the early morning in winter and really cold outside, and I couldn't sleep. I grabbed a blanket and went outside to the cold stone porch and sat on the steps in the back yard. It was probably 2:30 in the morning. I remember speaking to the Lord and telling Him all my feelings, and likes, and dislikes and how I thought He had turned His back on me, and I felt alone. I clearly remember looking up at the early-morning sky, and it was crystal clear and what seemed to be thousands of stars scattered all throughout the sky. I also unmistakably remembered there was not a single cloud across the sky. It was so clear that it surprised me. I glanced at the heavens and just stared into nothing. I turned away for probably 15 seconds because something caught my attention, but quickly turned back to look at the stars. To my complete amazement, the stars were gone and very heavy, thick clouds filled the sky. As a matter-of-fact there were so many clouds that not a single star was visible to the naked eye. It was just a very heavy over-cast.

At that very moment, the Lord spoke to me and asked the question 'Are the stars still there?' I said 'What?' He repeated the question, 'Are the stars still there?' 'Of course the stars are still there' I said. 'How can you be certain' He asked. Because I know that I know. Even so, you can't see them, He said, so how do you know they are there. 'Because the stars being present in the sky have nothing to do with the presence of the clouds. The stars are so much higher than the clouds.'

I mean here I am, all wrapped up in a blanket, in the back yard at 2:30-ish on a freezing winter morning, speaking to God, and being taught a lesson on stars and clouds, at least that's what I thought. It was really something much deeper as I looked back over the meeting we had.

Next God says, 'so although you cannot see the stars you are absolutely convinced that they are present, is that what you are telling me?' 'Yes,' I boldly said.

The next thing God said to me was, 'Am I still here?' 'Yes' I said not so boldly.' 'How do you know; you feel abandoned and alone' said God. 'I just know that you are here.' 'Are you absolutely convinced that I am present in your life like the stars are present in the sky asked God?' 'Yes,' I said, to which God said, 'That's good.'

Next time you want to do something, and you're not sure if anyone is watching you, and that soft gentle nudge in the spirit is prompting you not to do it, and you look to the left and to the right and all around you, I encourage you before you do anything, to look up, and don't be surprised when you hear 'Peek-a-boo my child, I see you.'

Prayer, Father, help me to realize when You told me You would never abandon me or forsake me, that You also meant that You would always be watching over my going out and coming in, and there would be nothing hidden from You that I do, say and think. Help me to touch bases with You before I do anything, and to trust You for the results.

Plop Plop, Fizz Fizz

Plop plop, fizz fizz, I know that if you're over a certain age, you will almost automatically fill in the rest of that sentence with, 'Oh what a relief it is.' How do I know? Because I asked a few older people if they remember what comes next, and they all remembered the little Alka-Seltzer character named Speedy. I also asked a few younger people, and they were clueless, you know; deer in the head-light blank gaze type of stare.

Plop plop, fizz fizz may work great on an up-set stomach, but it really can't do much for you when your life is seemingly out of control. We desperately look for anything to bring relief to that out of control feeling, only to find there are few solutions to life's roller-coaster rides, and a white tablet from a bottle is as far from the solution as the stars are from the earth.

What exactly is relief? It's help or assistance in an out of control situation. Bing tells us it's 'A feeling of cheerfulness or confidence and assurance that follows the removal of anxiety, pain, or distress.'

You see, my friend's relief; real and enduring relief will never be found in a bottle or a medicine cabinet. The best you can hope for is a momentary relief from the situation but as the word itself tells us, momentary means it's coming back again, and the thought of that doesn't really make you a happy camper

There is only one true source of relief in our lives, and when we allow God to be in control over our life, He takes away the stress and tension which is the best form of relief. How can He do that? Because you have abandoned the throne of your life, and allowed Him to take control of your life.

Why will God do this for us? Because we are told in Psalm 94:14 "For the LORD will not abandon His people, nor will He forsake His inheritance." In other words, our Heavenly Father wants only the best for us, His children.

This is why we are told in Isaiah 14:3 "On that day the LORD will give you relief from your suffering and turmoil and from the harsh labor forced on you." Again, in   Psalm 94:13 "You grant them relief from days of trouble, till a pit is dug for the wicked."

We see throughout the world so many examples of hurting people trying desperately to find relief from the harsh realities of life. Some turn to alcohol, others to drugs, and many to long hours of work. The problem is, these only masks or cover up the deeper rooted issues and never really address the root cause of the pain and suffering.

It's like a person who always has a headache, and they constantly take aspirin to mask the pain. Eventually, the aspirin brings about another medical issue and what was needed was to find out what caused the original headaches and deal with it. What the world is looking for is not temporary relief but permanent relief. The very thought of a re-occurring medical, or emotional, or mental problems are not something we enjoy looking forward to or even looking back over our shoulder at. In Job 35:9 we're told,

"People cry out under a load of oppression, they plead for relief from the arm of the powerful." It would seem that relief from situations is not only a personal issue but one that has been with mankind for as long as man has existed. Granted Philippians 4:7 states "That we will experience God's peace, which exceeds anything we can understand. His peace will guard your hearts and minds as you live in Christ Jesus." Although this is a reality, we seemingly seldom walk in that peace for very long only to find that the peace we experienced was a momentary relief.

So where does that constant relief from distress actually come from? Well, the good news is only the Prince of Peace can give the peace that we can walk in daily.

In John 14:27 the Prince of Peace tells us, "Peace I leave with you, my peace I give you. I do not give to you as the world gives. Do not let your hearts be troubled and do not be afraid." We're also told in Isaiah 26:3 "You will keep in perfect peace those whose minds are committed or dedicated to you, because they trust in you."

Who is the 'You' that this verse is speaking about? It's the Prince of Peace, Jesus himself. What is it exactly that Jesus is giving us? It's a peace which is true calmness, and tranquility, a time when there are no mental, emotional wars going on inside us, in other words, the condition of having no stress or conflict.

When it comes to real relief, plop plot, fizz fizz may work for a moment, but Jesus tells us, that 'He has given us His peace', and that it exceeds anything we can understand. He will keep us in perfect peace, or the lack of conflict, and all we have to do is keep our mind stayed or focused on Him, and the result is help or assistance in an out of control situation in our life.

Prayer, Father, You tell me that You have given me peace, but I find that my life is in pieces. Help me to keep my eyes focused on You, and realize that true peace can only come from the Prince of Peace, and if You gave it to me, then it belongs to me.

Running From God

Today's message is one in which the Lord woke me up and instructed me what to teach on, and it comes from the book of Jonah. It's also a lesson that I have personally experienced more than once, and I'm pretty sure some of you have either experienced it, or are going through it right now. It's called running away from the Lord. To be a little more specific, it's when the Lord calls you to do something that you don't want to do, so we run away. Oh yes, running away can take on many forms.

In Jonah 1:1 and Jonah 3:1, which is exactly the same, "Then the word of the Lord came to Jonah." The only difference is in chapter 3 it says, "A second time." To make it more personal, I like to leave the name Jonah out and ask you to fill in the blank with your name or a name of someone who is running away from the Lord.

You see; Jonah is very much like the rest of us, he's a reluctant missionary with the same word that we all get, 'GO!' Just to clarify something, I have heard so many tell me they have been called of the Lord, and I believe them.

To be called means you are called to be sent. Ask yourself, why would the Lord call you and not have you do anything with what He has called you to do? The problem is, we all like being called because it makes us think we're special, and we are, but we don't always like the sending part. It gets in the way of our plans, and our life, and our comfort zone, and our family time.

We read that the Lord told Jonah to go, and he did, 180 degrees in the opposite direction. My friends, we are no different than Jonah. The Lord asks us to do something that makes us uncomfortable, like tell your neighbor about the Lord, or share with your brothers and sisters about Jesus, and we run in the opposite direction because we don't want to make waves. Funny thing about the Lord, Jonah didn't want to make waves, so the Lord sent the waves to help change his mind.

As I said, running can take on many forms. In other words, we get so spiritually occupied in doing other things that we figure the Lord has to be pleased with all the things we're doing, and that He would never interrupt our busy schedule of doing things, to have us do what He wants us to do. In a nut shell, yes He will. You know the Holy Spirit is not a gentleman; He will make you comfortable when you're uncomfortable, and He will make you uncomfortable when you're comfortable.

This running away happened to me when I was living in Puerto Rico. The Lord, without permission mind you, broke into my calm life and asked me to do something that I really didn't want to do. So what I did was to get really busy with spiritual matters. I was part of every organization, and showed up to teach and preach at every opportunity. I figured; Lord look what I'm doing for You, You couldn't possibly want me to stop all this just to do what You want me to do. I was going around the mountain as they say.

One day, I even mentioned to the Lord about how busy I was to which He said, 'You are busier than I ever intended you to be. You're working from your talents, not from my gifts.' Boy, was that an enlightening experience. Did it change anything? Not a bit. I continued to run to every spiritual activity that I could find. Years later, a faithful brother said he had a word from the Lord, and I decided to record it. The word was 'That I have been going around the mountain so many times that I have packed the soil down and what was a small hill originally now became a very tall mountain.'

Did that get my attention? Yes, it sure did, because, deep down, within my spirit I knew I had a call from the Lord, and I knew that I had been running, and I knew that eventually my running from the Lord would have to end up with my running from the Lord to my running into the Lord. At that point, I had to lay everything at His feet, and pick up only what He wanted me to have. So, the word of the Lord came to Don, but Don ran and a second time the word of the Lord came to Don. Same word, different Don.

If you are running from the Lord, I suggest you just stop, because you can't win. Psalm 46:10 It tells us, "Be still, and know that I am God!" Another version says, "Stop your striving and recognize that I am God." That word 'Be still' means to cease from all your activity, and get to know your God.

Running from God and being busy in your talents may seem to be spiritual, but you will get burned out because you are busier than what He has intended for you. Don't get me wrong, God can and often times will anoint the work because He loves people, but you will find yourself exhausted and spiritually spent. Like a meteorite, you will be a bright light across the sky for a second only to end up as burnt out and used up. Running on the high octane of the Holy Spirit, you may get tired but never burned out.

Many of you know what I'm speaking about. You go on for hour after hour in ministry into the early-morning hours, and when it's over, you are so pumped with having been used by God that you could go on for many more hours, but you are physically tired, and that's normal, but you are not burned out because it wasn't you, it was the Holy Spirit in you.

My friends, if you are running from a word of the Lord, I suggest, you throw all your heavy baggage over board, throw your burdens over board, and lastly throw yourself over board to calm the storm that you have found yourself in and allow God to use you where He sends you. Truly, His grace is sufficient to keep you wherever He sends you. As it tells us in 2 Corinthians 12:9 each time He said, "My grace is all you need. My power works best in weakness. So now I am glad to boast about my weaknesses, so that the power of Christ can work through me."

If you want to be used of the Lord, His power works best in our weakness. Like Jacob, when you lose the battle, you really win, but if you win the battle, you really lose. In your own strength, you can do nothing, but as it says in 1 Corinthians 2:5 "So that your faith might not rest on human wisdom, but on God's power," and in Philippians 4:13 "I can do all this through him who gives me strength."

Running from God is an act of disobedience and defiance and how can God bless what He has already cursed. Stop running around the mountain and just say 'Here I am Lord, use me.' His grace, and His strength, and His power, and His faithfulness will be all you need to do whatever it is He asks you to do.

Prayer, Heavenly Father, deep within my spirit I know that You have called me to bloom where I have been planted, but, sometimes I get nervous about how I will be accepted, and I don't want to upset people. Help me to realize that You have called me for a reason, and have also given me everything I need to do what You have asked me to do.

Say What You Mean

I was reading in John 16:29 "His disciples said to Him, See, now you are speaking plainly, and using no figure of speech!"

The finest way to be understood is usually through communications, and although we are constantly surrounded by all forms of communications, from signs, to radio, to television, the best method is still in person speaking to one another.

I've found that if we are going to speak to one another say what you mean, and try to stick to the main point of the conversation and don't cloud the conversation so that what you are trying to say becomes lost in a jumble of needless words.

I remember when I was in college taking third-year physics, which was one of my majors, my professor, a graduate of M.I.T. was explaining a procedure to me, but although a wonderful physicist, he was a terrible communicator. As he continued to explain the procedure to me using large needless words, and way too many words, I just sat there like a deer looking into the head lights of a car with glazed over eyes, and tried to at least look like I was interested and understood what he was explaining to me. After 15 very long minutes, he was, thank God done. He asked me 'Well?' To which my only response was, 'I know that you were speaking English because there were a few words which I recognized from the English language, but truth be told, I have absolutely no idea what you were saying. The recognizable words were spaced too far between the unrecognizable words so that I couldn't join them together to make a complete sentence which made sense to me.'

Have you ever spoken to someone, so that when they got done speaking to you, you had no idea what they were trying to say? And although you were polite and smiled and said something intelligent like 'Wow or really, or amazing!' You still had no idea what they were saying, or where they were coming from, or how they felt about what they were trying to communicate to you. In other words, they were not speaking plainly to you.

We see exactly the same situation in John 16:29 "His disciples said to Him, See, now you are speaking plainly, and using no figure of speech!" Another version puts it this way, "His disciples said, "Now you're talking in plain words and not using examples." Another version says, "Then Jesus' disciples said, now you are speaking clearly and without figures of speech."

I don't know about you, but I personally find it frustrating when someone is speaking to me, and I have no idea what the other person is trying to say. Sometimes I feel like saying, just say what's on your mind and what you mean.

Don't get me wrong, I know there's often times a useful purpose in not coming directly to the point. Maybe the person you're speaking to is involved in something that they need to be made aware of, and they need to be spoken to in dark sayings or riddles or not clearly so they can pick out the truth and apply it to their own life and make the changes that need to be made. We see this in Numbers 12:8 with God Himself concerning Moses when we are told, "I speak with him face to face, plainly and not in riddles." Another version tells us, "I speak with him directly, openly, and not in riddles." We see this again in John 16:25, "Though I have been speaking figuratively, which means symbolically, a time is coming when I will no longer use this kind of language but will tell you plainly about my Father." In the God's Word version we are told, "I have used examples to illustrate these things. The time is coming when I won't use examples to speak to you. Rather, I will speak to you about the Father in plain words."

I understand there is a time and a place to speak using illustrations or riddles or even parables, but most of the time we are just speaking to one another, friend to friend, and face-to-face, and simple, clear communication is always best, there's really no reason to cloud the conversation with words that just don't seem to fit.

If you're angry at a person, in love just chose the right words, and let them know, and the reason why. If you're happy or pleased or proud of someone, just let them know. If you've been hurt, don't hold it in and let it fester and become a wedge in a relationship, let the person know, and get it behind you. How many times have we seen good friends become separated because someone said something the wrong way, and it was taken the wrong way, although what was said is not what the person meant, and a healthy friendship was destroyed?

And just the opposite, after many years of not speaking to what use to be your friend, the Lord prompts you to say something to the other person, and you are obedient, only to hear from your one-time friend, 'That's not what I meant at all, what I meant was,' and there's laughing or crying, hugs and a friendship is re-united because of a lack of understanding or misunderstanding of what was said.

My friends, the good news is we are not the only ones who fail to understand what's going on. In Mark 9:32 "But they did not understand what he meant and were afraid to ask him about it." In Luke 9:45 "But they didn't know what he meant. Its significance was hidden from them, so they couldn't understand it, and they were afraid to ask him about it."

I am so glad that the Father, the Son, and the Holy Spirit speak clearly too each of us, and not in dark sayings or riddles. When they speak, we know who's speaking, what they are saying and what our response needs to be. If, for some reason, we misunderstand what's being said to us, and we step out on the wrong path, thank God they can get our attention and speak into our lives a word of correction that will get us back on the right path to intimacy with God. How do I know this? Because 2 Timothy 1:9 tells us "God saved us and called us to be holy, not because of what we had done, but because of his own plan and kindness. Before the world began, God planned that Christ Jesus would show us God's kindness."

Prayer, Father, I ask that You would give me listening ears so that when You speak, I now Your voice, and know what my response needs to be. Give me discernment so when I hear voices that I'm not familiar with, I will be able to know the source and make the correct decisions that are pleasing to You.

Sin is Never a Good Idea

I was mediating on a phrase that I use often namely, sin will take you further than you ever intended to go, cost you more than you ever intended to pay and keep you longer than you ever intended to stay. As I was thinking about this phrase, I felt in my spirit to add another dimension to the statement, sin will hurt more people than you never intended it to hurt.

As I continued to mediate on this statement I was directed to read in Joshua 7:1 about the sin of Achan, where we are told "But the Israelites disobeyed the command about the city's riches. Achan son of Carmi, son of Zabdi, son of Zerah, from the tribe of Judah, stole some of the riches. The LORD was furious with the Israelites." In other words Achan sinned against what God had forbidden the men to do. By the way, sin is simply, breaking God's law. If God says 'Don't lie' and you lie, its sin. If God says 'Don't steal' and you steal regardless of the reason, its sin.

So here we have one guy, Achan, who is counted among the Israelites, and he decides to break God's law, and we find that this guy alone stole some of the riches, the things that God said 'Don't touch.' We are told in Joshua 6:18 "But stay away from what has been claimed by the LORD for destruction, or you, too, will be destroyed by the

143

LORD. If you take anything that is claimed by the LORD, you will bring destruction and disaster on the camp of Israel."

Can you imagine, one person sins and the entire camp of Israel is held accountable? Just so we see this in perspective, one man sins, and 600,000 men suffer the consequences.

What we read next just doesn't seem fair, but God's word is God's word, and He said stay away from what belongs to the Lord. We read in Joshua 7:3 "They returned and reported to Joshua, 'Don't send the whole army. About two or three thousand men are adequate to defeat Ai. Don't tire out the whole army, for Ai is small.'" Remember my friends, God was going before this army and it would seem that nothing could stop them, they were batting 1000 and no opposing army had been able to stand before them. But look what happens to the army of the Lord when they go in to this tiny town with their fierce warriors, we are told in Joshua 7:4, 5 "So about three thousand men from the people went up there, but they fled from the men of Ai. The men of Ai killed about thirty-six of their men, and pursued them from the gate as far as Shebarim and struck them down on the descent, so the hearts of the people melted and became as water."

Let's put this whole thing into perspective. One guy stole what God said 'Stay away from,' and if you don't stay away from it, not only you, but the entire camp of Israel will be held responsible, but not only responsible but liable for destruction.

Now I'm pretty sure that out of the 36 men that were killed that day by this tiny little insignificant army of Ai, there must have been a few that really loved the Lord, and trusted God, and went in to battle thinking 'This will be a piece of cake, after all, we defeated armies much larger and more fierce than this.'

You see my friends, sin will cost you much more than you ever intended to pay, and it will really hurt more people than you never intended it to hurt. Achan was probably thinking to himself that a few of the enemies' items can't hurt, after-all, no one will miss them with all this rubble and destruction all about. As a matter of fact in Joshua 7:20 we read, "Then Achan answered Joshua, 'It's true. I have sinned against the LORD God of Israel. This is what I did, I saw a fine robe from Babylonia, five pounds of silver, and a bar of gold weighing about one pound among the loot. I wanted them, so I took them.'"

So my question to you my friends is this, is a fine robe, 5 pounds of silver and a 1 pound bar of gold worth the lives of 36 innocent men? Men who were willing to give their lives in the service of the Lord? Of course not, but as I mentioned, sin will really hurt more people than you never intended it to hurt. I'm sure Achan never intentionally intended to have 36 of his fellow warriors killed. I'm also sure Achan never thought of the consequences of his actions, in other words Achan never thought of the consequences of sinning against God, who it would affect, and how it would end, which we read in Joshua 7:24-26, "Joshua and all Israel took Achan son of Zerah, the silver, the robe, the bar of gold, his sons and daughters, his cattle, his donkeys, his sheep, and his tent-everything he had-and brought them to the valley of Achor which means in Hebrew, disaster. Then Joshua said, 'Why did you bring this disaster on us? The LORD will bring disaster on you today!' And all Israel stoned Achan and his family to death. Then they burned the bodies and piled stones over them. They made such a large pile of stones over Achan that it is still there today. Then the LORD withdrew his burning anger. For this reason that place is still called the valley of Achor today.'" I have a saying, You can choose your choices, but you can't chose your consequences.'

My question to you my friends is, just because we are living in New Testament times under grace does that give us the license to sin against the very things that God has told us to stay away from? In 1 John 3:4 we are told "Everyone who sins is breaking God's law, for all sin is contrary to the law of God." Granted I John 2:1 tells us, "My dear children, I am writing this to you so that you will not sin. But if anyone does sin, we have an advocate who pleads our case before the Father. He is Jesus Christ, the one who is truly righteous."

Your sin can be forgiven according to 1 John 1:9 which says, "But if we confess our sins to him, he is faithful and just to forgive us our sins and to cleanse us from all wickedness." It doesn't tell us that there will not be consequences for our action of sinning against God. It doesn't tell us that we will not hurt many people by our sins, it doesn't tell how far our sin will take us until we finally get to the place that it's out of control and we need heavens help. It also doesn't tell us how much we will have to pay and how long it will take for the action of our sin to be forgotten.

So again my friends, be careful to stay away from those things that God is telling you to stay away from. I'm not going to personally make a list of what they are, we already know in our spirit what they are, and no matter how much we sugar coat them, they are still sin and breaking God's law.

Truly, sin will take you further than you ever intended to go, cost you more than you ever intended to pay, keep you longer than you ever intended to stay, and hurt more people than you never intended to hurt.

So rather than mention what the sins are, I'm going to point us to Galatians 5:16-26 which is telling each one of us, "So I say, walk by the Spirit, and you will not gratify the desires of the flesh. For the flesh desires what is contrary to the Spirit, and the Spirit what is contrary to the flesh. They are in conflict with each other, so that you are not to do whatever you want. But if you are led by the Spirit, you are not under the law. The acts of the flesh are obvious, sexual immorality, impurity and debauchery, idolatry and witchcraft, hatred, discord, jealousy, fits of rage, selfish ambition, dissensions, factions and envy, drunkenness, orgies, and the like. I warn you, as I did before, that those who live like this will not inherit the kingdom of God. But the fruit of the Spirit is love, joy, peace, forbearance, kindness, goodness, faithfulness, gentleness and self-control. Against such things there is no law. Those who belong to Christ Jesus have crucified the flesh with its passions and desires. Since we live by the Spirit, let us keep in step with the Spirit. Let us not become conceited, provoking and envying each other."

Can you agree with me when I say, 'Thank God we are not under the law?' I can't imagine disobeying God on one issue, and the consequences would have been me, my wife, my family, and everything I own, everyone in my family would be taken out to the edge of the camp, and put to death, and placed under a heap of stones such that my name would be as if it never existed. That is a sobering thought. Thank God for Jesus.

Prayer, Thank you Father that I am no longer under the law but under the grace of Jesus, and that when I sin against You, my sins can be forgiven, as long as I confess them and turn from them.

Stand On Your Own Two Feet

Have you ever found yourself in what seemed like a losing battle, and everything you did just seem to be of no avail? You tried to look at the situation through spiritual eyes and wondered how this was somehow going to be turned to good. You may have even told yourself that 'This whole mess wasn't even your fault, or you didn't start this thing.'

You probably felt like Joseph in Genesis 39:20 "So he took Joseph and threw him into the prison where the king's prisoners were held, and there he remained." My friends, it wasn't like Joseph was in prison a few days before the Lord started to move on Joseph's freedom. It tells us in Genesis 41:1 "When two full years had passed, Pharaoh had a dream." That's two full years in prison, and a prison is a prison, especially in Egypt with the summer heat, and bugs, and mice, and you probably slept on the floor on straw or hay. And why? Because someone lied about you, and someone had the power to throw you in prison, and you didn't deserve the punishment you got.

I would imagine; Joseph at times got really angry at the justice he received, and at other times asked God 'Why did you allow this to happen.' I'm also pretty sure Joseph didn't say to himself, 'One day I will be second in command of everything.' Joseph very likely didn't have a clue what was going on. If he recalled Psalm 37:23 "The steps of a good man are ordered by the LORD, and he delights in his way," Joseph was still in prison for nothing that he did and God apparently seemed far away from him just as God may seem to be far away from you while you are in your lion's den or your fiery furnace.

However, the truth is still the truth, and when we're going through anything that seems to be bigger than ourselves, we need to remember that God is in control, and although we may seem to be lonely in our times of trouble, we are not alone in our times of trouble.

As many of you know, I do not have a love of flying. Once a pilot asked me while we were in flight 'If I had a fear of flying' to which I responded, 'No, I have a fear of not flying.' One thing I use to tell myself, especially when we hit heavy turbulence was 'If I can't get out of a situation the next-best thing is to invite God into the situation.' Did the turbulence go away? Sometimes, but most of the time it didn't, and I knew that God had a purpose for me, and my life, and I knew it wasn't to be a statistic on a trans-Atlantic flight.

I said all that to say this, God's words to us are God's promises to us regardless if they seem to be working or not, and one of the many promises our Heavenly Father has made to us concerning the battles we face in life is found in Psalm 18:39 "For you equipped me with strength for the battle, you made those who rise against me sink under me." In other words, "Although you may seem like grasshoppers in your own sight" as we are told in Numbers 13:33, the truth is you are not grasshoppers next to the giants in your life, but you are ruthless giant killers in the hand of an Almighty God, who has equipped you with strength for the battle and has made those who rise against you sink before you. This is true regardless if you are able to see it with your eyes or not, because according to 2 Corinthians 5:7 "Indeed, our lives are guided by faith, not by sight."

We have all heard the expression, 'It's not over until the fat lady sings, or it isn't over till the fat lady sings.' It means that one should not assume to know the outcome of an event which is still in progress. More specifically, the phrase is used when a situation is or appears to be nearing its conclusion. It cautions against assuming that the current state of an event is irreversible, and clearly determines how or when the event ends. This would have been a great expression for Joseph when he was locked up in prison or for any of us when we find ourselves in a battle that seems to not only be out of control, especially our control, but that we are on the losing or defeated side.

One of the many things I've learned is, although God may seem not to be on time in delivering me out of my troubles, He is never late, and although I may really wish God would act the instant the problems start; He may, in fact, not move on my behalf until the very last second of the battle.

Why do you think God would act that way? Probably the same reason why when we were learning to ride a double wheeler bike, or we were teaching our children to ride a bike for the first time that we didn't step in and stop them from falling, so they could learn to balance themselves on their own, and like little children, God wants us to learn to balance and depend on Him, as Psalm 18:39 tells us, "For you oh Lord have equipped me with strength for the battle, you made those who rise against me sink under me."

When we get into that place of knowing that God has already done all that He has promised to do, we stand on our own two feet, and are able to rise up for any battle, just as we are told in Ephesians 6:13 "Therefore, put on the full armor of God, so that when the day of evil comes, you may be able to stand your ground, and after you have done everything, to stand."

Prayer, Father, sometimes things just seem to go wrong at the worst possible time during my life. Help me to keep my eyes on You and realize that as I do that, You will direct my steps, and You always have my best interests in mind, and You hold me in the palm of Your hand.

Where Is Your Hope?

Have you ever had one of those days when everything goes wrong? It doesn't make any difference how hard you try; it just seems that everything backfires on you? The harder you try, the worse it gets, and I'm convinced that all of us have had days like that.

I'll give you an example of what one of those days looks like, I heard a story, and I don't remember where it came from, about a lady at the airport who bought a candy bar to eat while she was waiting for her plane.

In the crowded waiting area, she saw an empty seat at the end of a row. Rushing to get it, she quickly placed her hang bag up against the end of the row, sat down, and placed her purse and several small items on the table between her and a rather large man seated there, and then turned back to straighten her hang bag.

With everything finally in order, she was ready to eat her candy bar. However, to her surprise, as she started to reach for it, she saw the man in the next seat to her unwrapping her candy bar, and she watched in utter amazement as he broke off a section and ate it.

She thought, "Well, my goodness, I've never seen such nerve." She glared at him, and he looked at her, but no words were exchanged.

She was so furious at what he had done that she decided that if he was going to be that rude about it, she could be just as rude, too. So she reached over to him, broke off a piece from the candy bar and ate it herself. Then he broke off another piece and ate it.

It became almost a duel between the two of them to see who would get the most. Quickly, the candy bar was consumed, and she sat there just boiling mad that someone would be so rude and so nervy as to eat half of her candy bar.

Well, after a few minutes of silence, the man got up and left and then came back with another candy bar. He unwrapped it, broke off a piece and started eating. She thought, "Well, since he ate half of mine, I'm going to eat half of his." So she reached over and broke off another piece and ate it.

Once again, the same scenario was repeated until the entire candy bar was gone. She sat there thinking, "This is the most ridiculous thing that has happened to me in my entire life." She continued to glare at him, and he looked at her, with neither one saying a word.

Just then, over the intercom came the announcement that her plane was ready for boarding. So she opened her purse to get her boarding pass and, to her utter embarrassment, there was her candy bar. She had eaten half of two of his candy bars, and her candy bar was still in her purse!

Things can go wrong and often times do go wrong, so with that, I was asking the Lord, 'What would be a good word to share with your children?''

Many topics came into my mind such as, the power of the believer, or who you are in Christ, or walking in victory and experiencing the supernatural.

All of these came to me but the more I thought about it, and prayed about it, the more I knew there was something else that was as important and that had to be shared.

With that, I heard, 'Where is your hope?' What is the definition of hope?

According to Bing, 'Hope is the emotional state which gives you the belief in a positive outcome in your life, or the feeling that what is wanted can be yours or that events will turn out for the best or to have a wish or to get or do something or for something to happen or be true.'

Those are definitions that the world uses, and although they are really good definitions, it still doesn't answer the question of what we hope for.

You may hope for enough money to pay the bills for this month. What about next month, or five months from now, or next year. Or you may hope to pass an exam in school, but what about next month's exam, or next year's exam?

The problem with hope is a lack of vision for the bigger picture. What do I mean? We often look at the wind or the waves in our lives, and hope they will stop. If they don't stop we get depressed, or angry, or frustrated, and want to give up, it's not worth it; we might think to ourselves. It could be a large wave or a little wave, a considerable problem or a little problem that causes us to want to give up. We lose hope. We lose vision for the bigger picture.

Could you imagine Paul in 2 Corinthians 11:25 where he tells us, "Three times I was beaten with rods, once I was stoned, three times I was shipwrecked, a night and a day I have spent in the deep?" What is the deep? It's the sea, an open ocean, and deep waters. A night and a day I was alone in the middle of an ocean.

Let me ask you, when was the last time you had beaten with sticks? Stoned and left for dead? Stuck in the middle of the ocean for a day and a night? If anyone had a good reason to give up and lose hope, it was Paul. However, he didn't. Why? Because he saw part of the bigger picture, he saw Jesus, and that He was in control.

Again, Paul tells us in Acts 14:19 "But Jews came from Antioch and Iconium, and having won over the crowds, they stoned Paul and dragged him out of the city, supposing him to be dead."

I personally don't know of anyone that has been stoned and dragged out of the city and left for dead.

When things go wrong, it's easy to lose hope. Look what Job says in Job 17:15 "Then where is my hope? Can you see any hope left in me?" Why did he say that?

Because everything that could go wrong with Job went wrong. Again, Job tells us in Job 19:10 "He beats me down on every side until I'm gone. He uproots my hope like a tree."

Let's face it, sometimes hope is the furthest thing from us. Sometimes you don't think that things will ever get better.

Well, I'm here to tell you; that is a lie from the pit of hell. Giving up on hope is a lie from the pit of hell.

Why would God say in Psalm 33:18 "The LORD's eyes are on those who fear him, on those who wait with hope for his mercy?" And again in Psalm 38:15 "But I wait with hope for you, O LORD. You will answer, O Lord, my God."

The enemy says, 'Lose hope in God and your situation' and God said 'Wait in hope for Him and His mercy.' There are 138 times that God says to wait for Him in scripture. If God says something just once it's important, but He says it 138 times.

You might be in the midst of a major crisis, but God is still in control. He controls the destinies of nations and men. Where is your hope? Is it on the moment that gets you out of your circumstance only to find that you may fall into again next week or next month?

Is your hope in your money that you could lose? Is it in your health that could fail you? Is it in your education? Where is your hope? If it's in anything other than the Lord God Almighty, you have a false hope because only God is faithful and will not, has not, and cannot fail.

You cannot be worried about your circumstances and trust God at the same time. You cannot be depressed, hopeless and discouraged and trust God at the same time You cannot be angry at people for your problems and trust in God at the same time Why? Because people are never your source.

If the Lord is your source, people can never destroy your destiny. If people could destroy God's destiny for your

157

life, then when God asks, 'Is anything too hard for Me,' the answer would have to be YES! However, since nothing is impossible for God, the real answer is NO! Therefore, God's destiny for your life cannot be destroyed as long as you keep your eyes on Him and stay close to Him.

It's easy to lose control, get depressed, and discouraged over things, and the enemy will help you to lose your joy.

Look what it tells us in Psalm 62:5-8 "I must calm down and turn to God; he is my only hope. He is my Rock, the only one who can save me. He is my high place of safety, where no army can defeat me. My victory and honor come from God. He is the mighty Rock, where I am safe. People, always put your trust in God! Tell him all your problems. God is our place of safety."

Where is your hope? The Psalmist tells us in Psalms 39:7 "So, Lord, what hope do I have? You are my hope." In other words, life with the Lord is an endless hope, but life without the Lord is a hopeless end.

Is there anyone who needs comfort? I know that there are. We lose loved ones; people lose jobs; some have physical problems; others are lonely and depressed, and some have financial issues. In other words, we experience all kinds of predicaments, but Jesus says that part of the solution to a troubled heart is trust, and He tells us to trust in three things.

Trust in My presence, trust in My promises, and simply trust in Me.

God is still in control of your out of controls, and He is still bigger than your biggest problem.

Prayer, Gracious, Heavenly Father, There are so many things that I have hoped for, and really wanted them to happen with my life, but many of my desires have not come to pass, and I was disappointed. Help me to always put my eyes on You alone, and to want only what You want me to want, for I know that in You, I will never be disappointed or ashamed, because I know that You are in control of all my out of controls.

Whine Doesn't Get Better With Age

Today's message is one of those times that allows me to become a little more visible and therefore, a little more vulnerable. I've noticed the greater my vulnerability due to being transparent, the greater the level to the relationship with my brothers and sisters.

If you're anything like me, and I hope there's at least one person that can relate to what I will be sharing on, and admit that this message is speaking to you as it has spoken to me.

Now for being transparent, when things don't go the way I would have liked them to go, or events happen to me that I really didn't want to happen to me, or I just didn't get my way; I have a tendency to complain or whine about the outcome. And the more I whine, the better I feel. Of course, nothing changes by my seemingly constant complaining. By the way, whining and complaining are basically the same thing. Complaining means to express dissatisfaction or misery about a situation, and whining is to complain in an unreasoning, repeated, or infuriating way. Just to be clear, there are a number of words that all mean the same thing, whine, complain, grumble and murmur.

Even if you try to spiritualize your complaining or grumbling, it's still something that we need to get away from because it isn't right, nor is it something people like to hear, and most important, God is not pleased with it.

As the Lord told me while I was having a full blown grumbling session all by myself, without another person in view, He said, 'Son, if you can complain about it, you can pray about it.' In 1 Corinthians 10:10 we're told, "And do not grumble, as some of them did--and were killed by the destroying angel." Well, that got my attention, and showed me there is a consequence for a life-style of grumbling. I guess that's why we are told in Philippians 2:14 "Do everything without grumbling or complaining." As a matter of fact, we are told in 1 Thessalonians 5:17 to "Pray without ceasing." If it told us to whine or complain without ceasing, many of us would have already arrived. Why is it that we always seem to fall into the area of complaining about events, people, or things that are not to our choosing or liking?

Have you noticed that most of our whining and complaining are aimed towards our friends, family or spouse who has nothing to do with the situation, and they really listen because they want to be polite, not that they are in agreement?

It would seem; we so easily forget what the Lord is trying to show us in unpleasant situations, and we end up in a state of grumbling, which, in reality, doesn't solve anything, and in most cases makes the situation seem so much larger than it actually is. In my life, and I'm sure in many of yours as well, when the prayers go up, the blessings come down. I really can't recall when the complaints or murmurs went up, and any blessings came down. Why? Because God doesn't favorably respond, or answer to complaints. In Numbers 14:27 it tells us "The LORD spoke to Moses and Aaron, saying, 'How long shall I bear with this evil congregation who are grumbling against Me? I have heard the complaints of the sons of Israel, which they are making against Me.'"

You see my friends; our complaints are not against the situation but against the Lord Himself. What we are actually saying is 'Lord, I don't like where you are leading me and guiding me.' Truth be told, if we are the righteousness of Christ, and the steps of the righteous are directed or ordered by the Lord, then we should learn to be satisfied with any situation that may arise in our lives. Paul said he learned to be content in every situation. Personally, I have no idea how long that learning curve took place. What I do know is, that I have not arrived at that place of being content in every situation.

An example of the consequences of murmuring can be found in Numbers 11:1 where we are told, "Now the people complained about their hardships in the hearing of the LORD, and when he heard them his anger was aroused. Then fire from the LORD burned among them and consumed some of the outskirts of the camp." Can you agree; the response from God due to our complaining is really not what we were looking for? We were looking for an answer for the problem but end up with something much worse than the problem.

Remember my friends, if you can complain about it, you can pray about it. The results of your prayers far exceed the results of your complaints. The greatest return from your investment comes about because of prayer.

We are told in Psalm 65:5 "You faithfully answer our prayers with awesome deeds, O God our savior. You are the hope of everyone on earth, even those who sail on distant seas." In Isaiah 65:24 we are again reminded of God's faithfulness in prayers and are told, "I will answer them before they even call to me. While they are still speaking about their needs, I will go ahead and answer their prayers!" Lastly, in Psalm 37:4 we read "Then you will take delight in the LORD, and he will answer your prayers."

Prayer, Father, sometimes, I admit that I am too quick to complain about the situations in my life or people in my life. Help me not to be a complainer, but one easily given over to prayer and depending on you when things don't go the way I would like them to go.

You Get What You Look For

On one of our trips back to Israel, I was confronted with a situation that could have become explosive if left to my own devices. Needless to say, the other individual didn't do what I would have liked them to do, and all I got was 'I'm sorry there's nothing that I can do; you have to speak with someone else.' Every person I spoke with concerning the problem told me, 'I'm sorry there's nothing I can do.'

From that point on, all I saw was what I looked for, and that was how useless the people were, and how incompetent they were to solve my problem.

A few days later, Norma spoke with the same person responsible, and he thanked us for our patience and gave us, not only what we requested but went the extra mile and gave us something much better than what we would have settled for. Once again, all I saw was what I looked for, but this time it was the professionalism and competent ability to resolve a situation to my liking.

As I thought about my attitude and behavior, it dawned on me that we get what we look for. In other words, if you are looking for the negative, you will find just that, or if you are looking for winds and waves in your midst, you will find just that. As a matter-of-fact, everything you see relating to the situations in your life will be shadowed with negative results, which will just add, as they say, gasoline to the fire. If, on the other hand, you look for the good in a situation, or in a person, you will find just that. You will see that there are a lot of good and positive possibilities in what was a negative situation. You will see that people really do try to solve problems, and help you if it's within their power to do so.

If I had taken the issue to the Lord from the very beginning, I would have saved myself so much grief in trying to get an outcome to a situation that was out of my control, and was always in God's control. I would have realized that Psalms 5:12 was speaking to me when it said, "Lord, when you bless good people, you surround them with your love, like a large shield that protects them." Again in Proverbs 2:8 I'm reminded that "He makes sure that people are treated fairly. He watches over his loyal followers."

You see; the word of God isn't true in just a few areas of your life where you have needs, but the word of God is true in every area of your life regardless if you have needs or not. When it tells us in Proverbs 30:5 "Every word that God speaks is true. God is a safe place for those who go to him." God himself tells us that every word that He speaks to us is true, the problem is we get caught up in the flow of the battle, and forget where our help comes from. This is why we are told in Ezekiel 3:10 "Then God said to me, Son of man, listen to every word I say to you and remember them."

Over and over again in scripture, God is telling his children to remember what He has told them. Since God never changes, He continues to remind us who are His children, to remember what he has been telling us. The word of God is amazing because it can be applied corporately, individually and personally.

165

If situations are looked at through the eyes of God, meaning that you put Him first, and commit all your circumstances into His hands, you will get what you look for, but it will be seasoned with God's presence. This is why Proverbs 3:5-8 says, "Trust the Lord completely, and don't depend on your own knowledge. With every step you take, think about what he wants, and he will help you go the right way. Don't trust in your own wisdom, but fear and respect the Lord and stay away from evil. If you do this, it will be like a refreshing drink and medicine for your body."

Back to my personal situation, immediately after I was told that there was nothing they could do for me, I leaned on my own understanding, and knowledge, and cleverness to get the results that I wanted, and I soon realized that I became part of the problem and not the solution. When we invited God into the situation, acknowledged Him in all our ways, He truly directed our footsteps, and the outcome was amazing, not only amazing but so much easier, complete and totally beyond what we could have done if we tried to imagine the best-case scenario for what we wanted. Once again, our Heavenly Father revealed that He is faithful and more than capable to direct our footsteps, just as He promised.

Prayer, Father, too often when things are not going my way, I try to take matters into my own hands, and lean on my own understanding to get what I want. That's when I become part of the problem, not the solution. Help me to trust in You and realize Your ways are always fair, and just, and right.

166

Who or What do You Trust In?

I was reading in Psalm 37:4, 5 "Take delight in the Lord, and he will give you your heart's desires. Commit everything you do to the Lord. Trust him, and he will help you."

As I was thinking about that verse, my mind was racing back to when I was about 9 years old, growing up in New York, and some of the things that I did as a child. As I look back over the years today, I have to admit that what I did then was not being brave but absolutely, and I hate to use this word, stupid, and the things that I put my trust in were equally as foolish and thoughtless, and what I thought was a successful mission then, was really the hand of the Lord protecting me and my life.

Once my best friends and I decided that if superman could fly so could we, and we got a rope and tied it off to a tree limb. The other end of the rope we tied to my belt after climbing to a second-story window of the building where I lived, and yes, I flew out the window, and thank God the rope didn't break. There I was a human pendulum, swinging back and forth until gravity stopped me. My best friend got up next, and we repeated the same death deifying maneuver, and thinking all along, what could possibly go wrong, and how very cool this was? One of the bullies about three years older than us was watching us and must have thought this was totally cool, and he wanted to try it. He just bullied himself right into the midst of what we were doing, grabbed the rope, tied it to his belt and jumped out the window. To make a long story short, the ambulance took him to the hospital with a few broken bones, and many scratches to prove that we were not designed to fly.

So the many questions become, who or what were we trusting in, or how cleaver we were, or how strong the rope was, or how cool it would be to fly? Today, 61 years after my flying out the window of a second-story building with a rope tied to my belt, I ask you my friends the same question. Who or what do you trust in?

Truth be told, there are many things that are competing for our attention to be the main thing that we trust. In the 1991 movie City Slickers directed by Ron Underwood and released by Columbia Pictures, Curly the cowboy helps us with making a choice by telling us, 'Let the main thing be the main thing.' Of course Curly was just an actor, and although there is much wisdom in what he said, our next question becomes, what is the main thing? Again Curly helps us by telling us, 'That's what you need to determine for yourself.'

Psalm 37:4, 5 takes our search a step further and tells us exactly who or what we are to trust in, "Take delight in the Lord, and he will give you your heart's desires. Commit everything you do to the Lord. Trust him, and he will help you."

The word that really jumped off the page at me in scripture is 'Trust.' The word trust, now that's a word that needs to be explained and understood. In Hebrew, it's the word batach baw-takh' and it means to have a confidence in, to be bold and secure in, to feel safe or made to be safe in and absolutely sure of.

It also has the connotation of believing in but not by blind faith, or having a warm fuzzy about. As a child, did I really and truly trust in that rope as I jumped out the window? Did I have a confidence in, or was I bold and secure, or did I feel safe and absolutely sure of the rope, or what I was about to do? Of course not, I didn't even think if the rope was strong enough, or what the consequences were if the rope broke.

168

All I thought about was the thrill of the adventure. That's why I said it was thoughtless. I didn't give any thought to what may have happened.

My friends, many of us have made decisions based on what we thought was trustworthy, and I'm sure, today, we tell ourselves, if I had to do it all over again, I would have never trusted in that person, or in that company, or even in my own decision. You may have even said to yourself, 'my final decision has come back to be part of the problem, and not the solution to what I thought was a good decision.'

Jeremiah 9:4 states, "Everyone must be on his guard around his friends. He must not even trust any of his relatives. For every one of them will find some way to cheat him. And all of his friends will tell lies about him." In Psalm 41:9, we read a similar situation, "Even my close friend, someone I trusted, one who shared my bread, has turned against me."

What happens when we trust in a government, since they are always there to help us, right? I'm pretty safe in not going down that road.

My friends, if we are going to have a confidence in something, and be bold and secure in something, and feel safe or made to be safe in and absolutely sure of something, that something has to be God and only God.

Don how can you say that with so many choices that are out there to trust in? I'm so glad that my telling you to trust in God, and only God is not an original statement.

Verses that support this are: "Those who know your name trust in you, for you, O LORD, do not abandon those who search for you." Psalm 9:10

"Trust and hope in him at every hour, oh, people, and pour out your hearts before him, because God is our refuge." Psalm 62:8

"But I am like an olive tree flourishing in the house of God; I trust in God's unfailing love for ever and ever." Psalm 52:8, and

"Trust in the LORD forever, for the LORD, the LORD himself, is the Rock eternal." Isaiah 26:4

So again the question becomes, who or what do you trust in? If it's yourself, friends, people in general, government or anything other than God Almighty, my suggestion would be to tread very lightly, research what you are told, and be careful. If, on the other hand, you trust in God for leading and directing your footsteps, and numbering your ways, then you are on a safe firm foundation for God Himself tells us, Isaiah 31:1 "Woe to those who go down to Egypt for help, who rely on horses, who trust in the multitude of their chariots and in the great strength of their horsemen, but do not look to the Holy One of Israel, or seek help from the LORD."

Prayer, Father, there are so many things to trust in, but help me to put my trust, confidence and faith in You for You are the One who leads me and guides my every step.

Whom Shall I Fear?

While reading in Psalm 27:1 which states "The Lord is my light and my salvation, whom shall I fear? The Lord is the strength of my life, of whom shall I be afraid?"

The New Living translation puts it this way "The LORD is my light and my salvation--so why should I be afraid? The LORD is my fortress, protecting me from danger, so why should I tremble?"

God's Word translation says, "The LORD is my light and my salvation. Who is there to fear? The LORD is my life's fortress. Who is there to be afraid of?"

So the question that ultimately has to be answered is 'What makes you afraid?' What are those things that keep you up in the middle of the night when everyone else is peacefully sleeping?

You know what I'm speaking about, those things that at 3:00 in the morning you are wrestling with, and wishing you were sleeping because you have to get up in a few hours to a full day of work. No matter, how hard you try to talk yourself to sleep, convince yourself that what you really need at this very moment is sleep, and the very last thing you are going to get is sleep.

Granted there are many things to be afraid of in the natural, things like disease, crime, failure, ecological disasters, and terrorism. Maybe you're in the middle of a court case that doesn't look like it's going in your favor, or there's a real crisis in your family with your children or your spouse and all the yelling and screaming doesn't make the problem any easier.

If the natural isn't enough, we also do battle in the spiritual, and that can keep us awake because of fear, concern, and expected problems.

Give you an example, when I worked at the Space Center, we were getting ready to go on our two-week Christmas break. My boss calls me into his office and says to me, 'When you get back from, your vacation, I want to see you in my office.' With that, he walks out the door to go on his vacation. In my mind, I went over every imaginable, and unimaginable thing I could think of. What did I do wrong turned into I need to think about a new job, I'm going to get fired for sure? I repented of things I didn't even do. In the night watch, it was a horror as I couldn't sleep, and tried to think of everything that I could have done wrong. After two weeks and completely worn out by the nightly wrestling matches, I went back to work. My boss calls me in and says this to me, 'Do you have that recipe for the eggplant parmesan that you made a few months ago?' All I could say was 'WHAT?!' 'You know, that eggplant parmesan that you made for us, do you have the recipe?' 'That's what you wanted? A recipe? You couldn't have asked me two weeks ago? Instead, you completely ruined my Christmas break. You owe me two weeks.'

What was I afraid of? That's easy, anything that could have gotten me fired from my job as an engineer on the space shuttle.

Where was God in the midst of all this? Same place He always is, just a prayer away waiting for me to call upon Him, and let Him be my light and my salvation.

Here in this Psalm we have David, who was no stranger to war and conflict in his kingdom. This verse shows us that David also struggled with fear.

You see, God wants to be involved in everything in our lives not just the hard times or bad times. He's God on the mountain top, and God of the valley. He's God when we have plenty, and God when we have little

The difference between David and me was David continued to meditate on God's strength, and in doing so was confident that whatever trials came his way, he would be safe and victorious. I meditated on the winds and the waves, and not He who calms the wind and waves.

David tells us the Lord is his light. In Hebrew that would have been the word 'Owr,' and it means illumination but not just to light up, but in every sense of the word, light of my happiness, light of life, light of prosperity, light of instruction, light of my face, just like Jehovah is Israel's light. As a matter-of-fact, that is one of the names of God, JEHOVAH-ORE "The Lord is Light"

In I John 1 we read, "This is the message we have heard from him and declare to you; God is light, in him there is no darkness at all." It didn't say God has light, but God is light.

Again in Isaiah 9:2 we read, "The people walking in darkness have seen a great light, on those living in the land of the shadow of death a light has dawned." The problem is not a lack of light but lack of a right choice. John 3:19 tells us "This is the verdict; Light has come into the world, but men loved darkness instead of light because their deeds were evil."

We have all heard it said that darkness is where things go bump in the night. Meaning this is where the fear comes from, the scary stories come from, and the superstitions come from, but we are not of the darkness because we have

173

the Light within us, and this is why David said, 'Whom shall I fear?' In other words, I'm not afraid of the darkness, the unknown, and the things I do not know. I'm not fearful of the enemy outside or the enemy inside.

It's like in the 1954 book The Lord of the Rings by J.R.R. Tolkien when Alanon was about to confront a very evil darkness, he said 'I fear no man.' Of course his lack of fear was in his determination, but the believer's lack of fear is in the Lord, after all didn't He say that 'He has not given us a spirit of fear.' Well if He didn't give it to us, and we have it; the question is, where did it come from and why are you accepting anything from anyone other than the Lord?

Like David, our motto should be 'The Lord is my Light, and He dispels all fear and confusion and uncertainty and darkness.' Knowing that our bold proclamation should be, whom shall I fear? The answer is, I fear no man, no darkness, no confusion, no enemy and no uncertainty.

Prayer, Gracious Father, often times I find myself fearful because of the many things that have come into my life which I have absolutely no control over. I know that You have not given me a spirit of fear, and I would ask You to help me to realize that You are still in control of my out of controls, and with You on my side, I have no reason to fear anything that comes my way, because I trust in You.

The Dove and the Scorpion

I had a word from the Lord the other day to do a teaching on the Dove and the Scorpion. I wasn't sure what the dove, and the scorpion were about until the Lord revealed it to me. I'm certain many have heard similar versions of this story, but I heard specifically Dove and Scorpion, so here goes.

One day, there was a scorpion that needed to cross a large river. He had no way of getting to the other side and there was urgent business that the scorpion needed to take care of. He was well aware of the fact that if he attempted to swim to the other side, he would be eaten by large fish or carried downstream by the fast-moving current. He also knew that it would take almost forever to find a spot where he could cross over safely. So as he stood there on the shore saying to himself, what to do, what to do. A dove flew by, and he called out to the dove. Excuse me dove he called out, and the dove landed right next to the scorpion. What can I do for you, she asked? I have an extremely pressing matter on the other side of the river and for me to walk or swim to the other side would be extremely dangerous or take forever for me, so I was hoping that you would allow me to crawl upon your back and for you to fly me to the other side. I'm sure it would only take you a very, very short time, and I hardly weigh anything. I don't know said the dove; you are a scorpion, and your type has a terrible reputation for that deadly stinger at the end of your tail, and I would be very fearful that you might sting me. I give you my solemn promise that I would at no time sting you, besides if I did it would mean the death of both of us and why would I do something like that when I'm in such a hurry. The scorpion went on and on about how he would never do anything like that until the dove was won over by the convincing scorpion. So he crawled up on the back of the dove and off they went. Halfway across the river the scorpion for no reason at all stung the dove with his deadly tail, dooming both to a sure death. The dove as she was getting weaker from the venom from the stinger asks the scorpion, why would you do that, why would you sting me after you made all those promises, and after I agreed to help you on your quest to the other side? I'm really sorry commented the scorpion; it was really not my intention but stinging others is who I am and what I do, and I couldn't help myself.

There are so many things to say about this story, so many life issue choices to look at. Even more important, there are so many situations into our lives where this story becomes so true. In 1 Corinthians 15:33 "Bad company corrupts good character." In Deuteronomy 23:6 speaking about the wrong people to associate with, we are told, "Do not seek a treaty of friendship with them as long as you live." Some of the best examples come from Psalms, in Psalm 109:5 we read "They repay me evil for good, and hatred for my friendship." In Proverbs 12:26 "The righteous choose their friends carefully, but the way of the wicked leads them astray."

I read a teaching the other day from Mark where Jesus warned us to be careful about deceptions. Who was Jesus speaking to? Certainly not unbelievers because their entire life is nothing but deception. How can I make that statement? Jesus said in John 14:6 "I am the way and the truth and the life." If you are not going the right way, you are being deceived, if you are not walking in truth, you are being deceived, and if you are not living a full life, you are being deceived. In other words, everything about Jesus is right and correct, and there is no deception in Him. If you follow Him you are not being deceived, and if you are not following Him you are being completely deceived.

176

So back to the part about bad company corrupts good character, and wrong friends, and having good friends.

To be sure, there are numerous more verses that speak about how the choice of friends can be a snare or stumbling block down the road.

One more thing, if your friends are not encouraging you to the deeper things of God, be careful. Having a friend who complains about the world situations, or governments being out of control, or gossip about what's going on is not what you want to hear, you already know that, what you need to hear is how to get closer to the Lord, and how to press into the deeper things of God.

I'm certain many of us have either heard about or experienced firsthand how being associated with the wrong company has led to a season of problems and misfortune. I'm also sure that there were many promises of, 'It's okay, trust me nothing can go wrong,' or 'I've done this many times before, and it's fun' or how about 'Would I ask you to do something that was dangerous?'

We were told earlier that bad company corrupts good character, and it's there for a reason. Bad company really does end up corrupting the Christ like morals and standards that we have come to not only rely upon, but to put our confidence in.

Another expression that always seems to pop-up after the facts is, 'My intentions were right', to which I respond, 'The road to hell is paved with good intentions.'

I believe the Lord had me use the dove because it is a symbol of peace and tranquility, and has always been associated with the children of God and innocence. We read in John 1:32 "Then John gave this testimony, "I saw the Spirit come down from heaven as a dove and remain on him." However, in Revelation 9:5 we're told, "They were not allowed to kill them but only to torture them for five months. And the agony they suffered was like that of the sting like a scorpion when it strikes."

I believe it's very clear that doves are associated with life, and scorpions are associated with death and agony. As children of the Living God, I strongly recommend that you not only choose life, but associate with vessels of life and stay as far away from anything that is not of God because those of darkness are what they are, causing them to do what they do. I'm not saying do not witness to those of darkness, we are called to witness to the lost, but I am saying don't let their ways influence your actions.

I once read a text illustration by Saeed Richardson from Sermon Central of a little boy wanted to meet God. He knew it was a long trip to where God lived, so he packed his suitcase with a bag of potato chips and a six-pack of root beer and started his journey.

When he had gone about three blocks, he met an old man. He was sitting in the park, just staring at some pigeons. The boy sat down next to him and opened his suitcase. He was about to take a drink from his root beer when he noticed that the old man looked hungry, so he offered him some chips. He gratefully accepted it and smiled at him.

His smile was so pretty that the boy wanted to see it again, so he offered him a root beer. Again, he smiled at him. The boy was delighted! They sat there all afternoon eating and smiling, but they never said a word.

As twilight approached, the boy realized how tired he was and he got up to leave, but before he had gone more than a few steps, he turned around, ran back to the old man, and gave him a hug. He gave him his biggest smile ever.

When the boy opened the door to his own house a short time later, his mother was surprised by the look of joy upon his face. She asked him, "What did you do today that made you so happy?" He replied, "I had lunch with God." But before his mother could respond, he added, "You know what? He got the most beautiful smile I've ever seen!"

Meanwhile, the old man, also radiant with joy, returned to his home. His son was stunned by the look of peace upon his face, and he asked, "Dad, what did you do today that made you so happy?"

He replied "I ate potato chips in the park with God." However, before his son responded, he added, "You know, he's much younger than I expected."

Too often we underestimate the power of a touch, a smile, a kind word, a listening ear, an honest compliment, or the smallest act of caring, all of which have the potential to turn a life around. People come into our lives for a reason, a season, or a lifetime! Embrace them all.

Prayer, Lord, there are so many wolves in sheep's skins in the world, and I would ask You to help me with discernment and sensitivity to know who and when to trust in those who I come in connection with in business or even my social circle.

ABOUT THE AUTHOR

Even as a young boy Don Honig knew that there was always something that was much bigger in life but had a hard time trying to understand what it was.

Growing up in New York City in a Jewish home, things of a spiritual nature were not encouraged and asking questions about the Lord Jesus Christ was definitely frowned upon and strictly unmentionable in the home.

Much later in life, Don tried to disprove many of the deeds that Jesus Christ claimed, and in order to do that, Don started to read the bible, Old and New Covenant. The Old Covenant was somewhat familiar with many of the names of the individuals found there, but the New Covenant became a real challenge and eventually Don was faced with a major crisis. He either had to accept or deny the many claims that Jesus made. The dilemma was; all the claims were true and Don couldn't deny the truth and had no choice but to joyfully accept the Jewish Messiah as his personal Lord and Savior.

It is the desire of Don Honig to speak the Word of God through the power of the Holy Spirit and to see the captives set free; the blind receive their sight and the deaf to hear the good news.

Don will continue by the leading and guiding of the Lord to bring people out of darkness and death into God's glorious light and life through the Word of God with demonstrations of signs and wonders.

Don's first book, When God Invades Your Everyday Life, is a 52 week devotional revealing that the Lord God Almighty, is also a God that enjoys revealing His presence to His children in the everyday situations of our lives.

72002401R00104

Made in the USA
Columbia, SC
10 June 2017

To the Brinkley family. May you experience the manifested presence of Jesus Christ in all that you do

Don Honig

THE GOD WHO WALKS WITH HIS CHILDREN

Practical Day-to-Day Experiences With God

Donald E. Honig